FLY TYING with Poly Yarn

BOB LONG JR.

Lee Clark and Joe Warren

Frank Amato PORTLAND

Dedication

First and foremost to our Lord and Savior, Jesus Christ. To Him be the glory.
In memory of my parents, Ted and Gladys Clark, who instilled in me
a love for the great outdoors and, most of all, took me fishing.
To my wife Betty, who encouraged me to not let my many hobbies dominate our lives.
To my son Gerry, my number one fishing partner and fly tester.

—Lee Clark

To my wife Melissa and children, Yoshie, Ashley, and Katy Warren,
whom I am indebted to for time spent away from them.

— Joe Warren

Acknowledgments

To Frank Thill, whose fly, "The Getter," directly inspired the creation of Clark's Stonefly. Gerry Tinkle, for teaching me a lot about writing. Without his encouragement, I wouldn't have attempted to write this book. To Greg Richards, fishing partner and close friend, whose support and encouragement goes beyond this book. John Shewey, for writing the first magazine article about Clark's Stonefly, and contributing the Foreword for this book. To Gary Kish, for being one of the first ambassadors of the Clark's Stonefly. Bob Long Jr., who was gracious enough to do the cover photograph.

To the fly tiers who graciously contributed their patterns: Tim Borski, Charlie Boyce, Chuck Brunham, Keith Burkhart, Chuck Cameron, Gerry Clark, Alan Cline, Duane Dunham, Ken Hanley, Henry Hoffman, Bob Long Jr., Mike Marchando, Chris Mihulka, Bill Myers, Aaron Ostoj, Ed Rizzolo, Ken Taylor, and Greg Webster. Thank you for sharing your talents.

To Jim Schollmeyer, for his wonderful photography of the fly plates. To Frank Amato and his staff, for accepting this project for publication and fine-tuning it.

To all the writers, store proprietors, and anglers who helped make the Clark's Stonefly popular, and in so doing made this book possible.

—Lee Clark

Frank Amato Publications, Inc.
P.O. Box 82112, Portland, Oregon 97282
503•653•8108   www.amatobooks.com

Illustrations by Lee Clark.
All photography by Joe J. Warren unless otherwise noted.
Individual flyplate photography by Jim Schollmeyer
Cover photography by Bob Long Jr.
Flies tied and originated by Lee Clark unless otherwise credited.
Book and Cover Design: Kathy Johnson
Printed in Singapore
ISBN: 1-57188-201-4   UPC: 0-66066-00415-4
1 3 5 7 9 10 8 6 4 2

Table of Contents

BOB LONG, JR.

"The Clark's Stonefly is one of the
most effective patterns for imitating hatches of
golden stoneflies and salmonflies. Its combined
traits of durability, floatability, effectiveness
and ease of tying are unmatched by any
other patterns I've used . . . I spend
more time fishin' and
less time fussin'."

—Gary Kish, 1986

Foreword

FOR THE ANGLER WILLING TO LOOK beyond the fly's obvious "fishability," Lee Clark's Stonefly exemplifies the creative, evolutionary process by which most snippets of feather and fur find themselves arranged upon an angling hook. Lee's single-minded dedication to devising a more effective stonefly pattern derived from his dissatisfaction with the flies which he first fished over hatches of these insects. His creativity fueled by chance encounters with other anglers—whom he readily credits for inspiring his efforts—Lee combined elements from a variety of other flies. Added to these design elements was a peculiar material that Lee had stumbled upon for purposes unrelated to fly dressing. His mind predisposed to occupy itself with thoughts of fly design, Lee made the connection between his desire for a better stonefly and the macramé yarn he had used in his school teaching. Born that day was the Clark's Stonefly: A classic story of fly evolution and development.

Having said all that, I hasten to add that the "fishability" part remains impossible to ignore. Plain and simple, Clark's Stone ranks amongst the best of the dry (sometimes "damp") patterns for imitating stoneflies. The fly becomes increasingly valuable as the trout become increasingly jaded to more traditional offerings. Such is the mark of an effective fly. For my money the greatest of them all is Cal Bird's remarkable stonefly: Having survived the test of time, the Bird's Stone, when properly tied, fishes beautifully under all conditions and retains a truly artistic quality at the hands of an accomplished tier. Herein, however, lies one of Lee Clark's secrets for success: A tier of any skill level can easily master the Clark's Stonefly, arriving at a fly that may well be the fishing equal to the intricate Bird's Stone.

This concept of simple effectiveness permeates all of the Lee Clark patterns derived from the original stonefly. These flies and the techniques used to dress them are outlined in this valuable reference. Surely there exists an inherent value to artistic, challenging fly dressings; yet just as certain is the pragmatic value of flies that are simultaneously simple and effective. Lee Clark has mastered this certainty; mastered the craft of developing patterns that are easy and quick to tie and at the same time deadly effective astream.

—*John Shewey*

Introduction

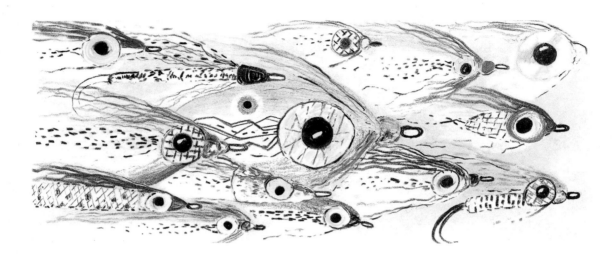

THIS BOOK WOULD NOT EXIST IF IT weren't for the creation and evolution of the fly pattern called "Clark's Stonefly." It is a simple pattern which constitutes only four materials, the most essential one being polypropylene yarn. It was originally designed to fill a personal fishing need. Over the years, its trout-catching reputation grew steadily through word of mouth, the media, fly-tying exhibitions, and the computer world. As a result, I felt I should document the experience of where the Clark's Stonefly has taken me and share it with you.

I was first introduced to polypropylene yarn as macramé cord over twenty years ago as a teacher instructing a high school art class. One particular project in my class was having my students craft wall hangings, plant hangers, decorative owls, etc., from macramé yarn, to teach them the art of knot tying. To add the finishing touch to the bottom of most of the projects, the cord ends were brushed out. It was this fuzzy finished appearance that prompted me to consider its application in fly tying and soon after,

the development of my special pattern, Clark's Stonefly. To my knowledge at the time, poly yarn was primarily sold as a craft material.

The history and science behind the production of poly (short for polypropylene) yarn is an interesting one. Polypropylene entered commercial production in 1957, and is one of the fastest growing thermoplastics of all. It can be tailored to many fabrication methods and applications especially for fiber and filament, film extrusion, and injection molding. Other types of polypropylene products include apparel, upholstery, carpets, packaging material for cigarettes, candy, and potato chips. It is used to manufacture automobile trim and even house siding. To say the least, it is a very versatile material that comes in many forms that are both strong and durable.

Macramé cord is 100% polypropylene, just like the plastic mentioned previously. It is a synthetic material which not long ago was barely acknowledged in fly tying as natural fibers were predominant. Synthetic yarns were probably

some of the first materials of their type to be used in fly tying. Currently there are many synthetic materials for fly tiers to choose from, they are growing popular in fly tying as tiers research new ways to use them. Looking specifically at the synthetic yarn section alone, there are many listed bearing trade names such as: Antron, Antron Sparkle Yarn, Antron Yarn, Wool-Style, Z-Lon, Zelon, Poly Yarn, and of course Clark's Tying Yarn.

Other additions to the poly yarn tying list include Aqua Fibers and Poly Bear. Both are 100% polypropylene. Aqua Fibers is available in many colors, with some colors conveniently mixed. Poly Bear is very appealing with thin strands of tinsel added for flash. I for one have to admit that this addition has greatly improved polypropylene as a fish-catching material.

One question I am frequently asked at fly-tying exhibitions is, "What is the difference between Antron yarn and Clark's Tying Yarn (100% polypropylene)?" Each is manufactured the same, but with a

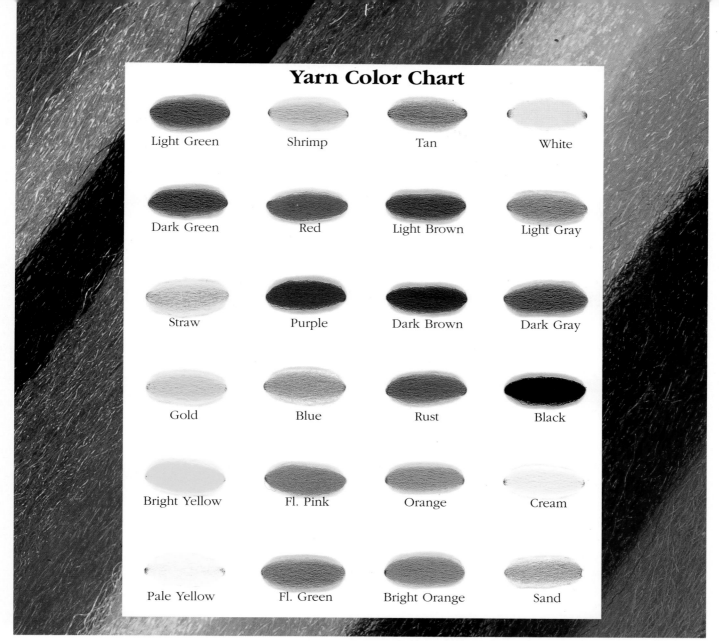

Yarn Color Chart

Light Green	Shrimp	Tan	White
Dark Green	Red	Light Brown	Light Gray
Straw	Purple	Dark Brown	Dark Gray
Gold	Blue	Rust	Black
Bright Yellow	Fl. Pink	Orange	Cream
Pale Yellow	Fl. Green	Bright Orange	Sand

different set of chemicals. Visually, even with a very strong magnifying glass, the two appear to be similar, but the polypropylene filaments look and feel slightly larger in diameter and are rougher in texture. Since the texture is different it will make a difference in how it is used when tying. Antron is popular for wings and simple body wraps. The rigidity and coarseness of poly yarn offers more stability, and as I have found over the years that like other materials it can be manipulated by twisting, dubbing, or spinning to obtain special effects.

Macramé cord is available in craft stores but most fly tiers don't need fifty yards of cord. For manageable amounts of poly yarn in convenient fly-tying packaging, check your local fly-fishing shop for Clark's Tying Yarn. Each package contains five yards of ready-to-use yarn. The chart on this page features the most-used colors for your fly-tying needs.

Poly yarn for tying flies is an excellent material because it is easy to use, durable, and effective. "Easy" because it's a no-brainer to tie with. "Durable" because the material holds together well without coming apart at the vise, not too mention false casting and slashing fish bites. "Effective" because no matter how you tie with it, it serves its purpose, and finally, it generates fly patterns that fish will eat! The yarn is very forgiving to work with no matter how little tying experience you have. It can be applied on all patterns, dry or wet, fresh or salt water! Its only limitations are the extent of your creativity.

When it comes to fly tying and fishing, I am a creative individual who always looks for new and nontraditional ways of doing things. Poly yarn is definitely the answer when it comes to completing a quick and simple, fish-catching fly right out of the vise. I know you will enjoy this book and discover that Clark's Stonefly is not just another fishing fly but an example of what can happen over time, with a very simple idea.

Lee Clark
St. Helens, Oregon
February 2000

Chapter One

Tying Techniques For Poly Yarn

BEGINNING IN THE WINTER OF 1983, the Clark's Stonefly was the first pattern I tied using the poly yarn. The poly yarn was used in a very simple fashion for the body like a down wing material. This easy concept started an evolution of many patterns, and is only one of many easy tying techniques.

For me, developing resourceful tying techniques with the same type of material is what makes the whole tying game interesting. For about the last decade I have performed at fly-tying shows and this has prompted me to develop something a little bit different from the year

before in my tying demonstration. As a result I have created some interesting bugs, and their simplicity has made doubters into believers.

I like using poly yarn very much, in case you couldn't tell. When I'm on a fishing trip and have to be ready to match the hatch, all I need are some different colors of yarn, a couple of hackle patches, and some thread. The yarn's texture is perfect—not too coarse, not too soft. The diameter of the single fiber makes the density of yarn easy to experiment with when you need to adjust for wings, tails, bodies, etc. The yarn does-

n't take a lot of time to prepare it for tying. It is bouyant, blendable, and buggy.

I began with four colors: yellow, gold, rust, and orange. These were hot colors for Clark's Stonefly and variations from these colors were further expanded by combing them together. New patterns from different tying methods increased color selection. For example, twisting yarn to form a spiral body opened doors to making damselfly bodies. Light blue was added to the list. Fluorescent colors have attracted steelhead tiers. The number of colors has increased to 24. Poly yarn has become a universal material for all types of fly tying. This chapter discusses creative uses for poly yarn developed after many years of experimentation through trial and error. The nice thing about polypropylene yarn is it can be fashioned in many ways. Used straight, it can be a durable shellback material. It can be dubbed then picked out to imitate life like legs. A bundle of straight filaments can be twisted then wrapped to suggest a segmented body. The body of a caddis pupa can be imitated simply by dispersing a small bundle of yarn around a hook to form a skirt. Finally, the yarn can be fashioned into any desirable color of dubbing.

Technique #1: Combing and Mixing Yarn

The most important preparation when tying flies with poly yarn is combing the fibers to a ready state for tying (some poly yarn tying products do not require combing). For example, if one were to look at Clark's Tying Yarn right out of the package, it's kinky and curled fibers are unpleasant to say the least. However, once you start to stroke a comb through the lifeless fibers they immediately straighten out and open brightly! Brushes are not usually recommended because they tend to fray and tatter the poly fibers making more of a mess than an asset for tying. The best comb to use is one that has two different styles of combing teeth, such as a fine-tooth and a wide-tooth pattern. Larger quantities of poly yarn can be combed with the wide-tooth comb, smaller amounts with the fine-tooth comb.

Combing is also an excellent way for blending colors. From mixing basic colors together you can create a variety of natural tones for matching insect colors such as olives, browns, and tans.

Step 1: Start with one or two strands of yarn, firmly grasping the ends with your left hand (assuming right-hand dominance). Insert the comb into the fibers using the fine-tooth portion at slightly less than a 90-degree angle. If

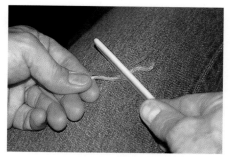

you use too much of an acute angle to comb with, the yarn will immediately bind up in the teeth. If this happens pull the comb out and use the wider-tooth pattern or tease the fibers apart with your fingers. When you can stroke the comb smoothly through the fibers revert back to the fine-tooth comb. Always use slow and even combing strokes to minimize tangling and knotting of the yarn.

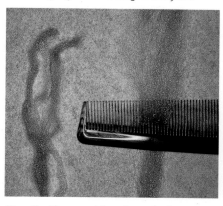

Step 2: After combing through the yarn it should have a straight, fluffy look to it. Note the difference of before and after the yarn is combed.

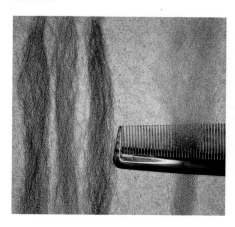

Step 3: Combing also helps blend different colors together although you should also tease apart and mix the fibers by hand and make a few more strokes of the comb to bring the fibers back into a single strand again. Examples of blending different colors

are (from left to right): black/gray, gold/brown, olive/brown, and gold/orange in the comb.

Technique #2: Blending Yarn for Dubbing

Poly yarn can easily be made into a dubbing material with the use of a coffee blender. Even without a blender, you can still create a dubbing loop and apply combed and cut short pieces of yarn for an aggressive buggy appeal (refer to tying steps of the Brillo Bug, page 37). But from a blender, the mixed concoction of poly yarn and natural hair achieves a nice balance of a coarse and pliable dubbing like none other. Soft textured hair (like rabbit) adds substance to the poly yarn and makes the best blend. Even hair shed from a dog works great, Lee's golden cocker spaniel proved it!

Step 1: Comb 5 to 6 inches of poly yarn and begin trimming into short pieces about 3/4 of an inch long.

Step 2: Add about the same amount of natural hair or fur to the poly yarn. Experiment with different ratios of the natural and synthetic blend to determine your own favorite blend.

Step 3: Begin mixing the fur and yarn back and forth a few times by hand and then place into a coffee-size blender (preferably a blender dedicated only to fly tying). Only use

a few short bursts of the blender to mix the contents up. Over-blending causes the poly yarn to become burned and over-stretched, after all it is a form of plastic.

Step 4: The end result should be a nice even blend of poly dubbing ready for thread-core direct dubbing or a dubbing loop.

Technique #3: Molding Poly Yarn

The use of glues in fly tying to fabricate parts of the fly's shape has practically become an art of its own. For many years the most popular adhesive, epoxy, has been demonstrated in tying saltwater patterns. Even silicone and hot glue have made their claim in fly tying. Adhesives have contributed many attributes to fly tying such as a more durable fly, realistic imitations, and a transparent finish that enhances the look of coated materials.

The recent introduction of a new glue product has brought poly yarn to yet another level of fly tying creativity. It is called Soft Body (by Angler's Choice), and is manufactured with fly tying in mind as a non-toxic, water-based plastic resin. The resin is made in thick or thin viscosity. Soft Body is clear, dries relatively quickly, and when used on poly yarn is pliable and strong. It can also add to the buoyancy on surface flies,

especially when coating a body of yarn with a hollow core (refer to Soft Body Plopper, page 38).

Step 1: Comb the desired color(s) of yarn to be used. Use a plate of Plexiglas or wax paper to work on (any hard surface that the glue will not immediately adhere to). Anchor down one end of the yarn. With your free hand, use your index finger and dab a fair amount of Soft Body on the yarn. Apply several dabs along the yarn replenishing each dab of resin as you apply it to the yarn.

Step 2: With your index finger, stroke the surface of the yarn spreading the Soft Body evenly over the surface and pushing it into the yarn fibers.

Step 3: Mold the strip of yarn by stroking it with your thumb and index finger. This will help shape the width and density of the yarn.

Step 4: Allow the resin to set up and harden. You can use a lamp to speed up the process of drying. It may be cured in several hours.
Step 5: The yarn should be well hardened

into a beef jerky-like strip. Note: The density of the strip will depend on the amount of yarn you use and how much you spread the yarn apart when flattening the fibers with the resin.

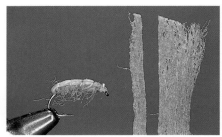

Step 5a: Yarn strip used as the shell back on a poly scud pattern.

Step 5b: Notched yarn strip to shape wing case on stonefly nymph.

Step 5c: Very thin yarn strip cut to shape realistic wings on Clark's Stonefly.

Technique #4: Yarn Foundations

Forming a foundation to support, divide, or lift tail and wing materials is very important in order to prevent fouling or wrapping of such body parts around the hook when it is fished. Another consideration is how the fly will ride or keel if it is fished in a trolled or retrieved fashion. It is highly essential that materials like marabou or splayed hackle tips maintain their freedom to elicit a natural movement indicative of their imitation.

The poly yarn has the right consistency for forming excellent foundations, it's not too limber and not too rigid. Most likely, you will have to experiment with the amount of poly yarn to use to construct the desired foundation.

Splayed Tail

This example illustrates the foundation for splaying hackle tips as seen on a tarpon fly. The same foundation can be used for any tail material that is tied atop the bend of the hook.

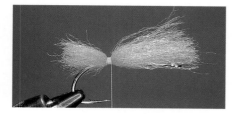

Step 1: Cut 5 strands of yarn (if using Clark's Tying Yarn) to about an inch and a half long. Add a thread base to the hook where you will tie in the tail. Before tying the yarn in place, have the thread in a starting position where it hangs midway between the hook's barb and point. Place the yarn over the thread wraps, push fibers over and around the shank covering it completely. Hold the yarn in place with your index finger and thumb and wrap the yarn over with one or two loose wraps, then tighten the wraps as you apply more. The yarn tips should barely exceed the hook's bend. Trim to the correct distance if needed.

Step 2: Turn the hook upside down to make sure the yarn is completely surrounding the shank. If not, unwind the thread to the last wrap (hold on to the yarn) and try rolling the

fibers further around the shank by pushing with the thread as you wrap around it.

Step 3: Tie in the hackle tips on each side of the yarn with the feathers dull-side facing out. The hackles should have a natural curve or splayed fashion as pictured. The yarn will prevent the hackle tips from fouling around the hook or with each other and enhances the closing and opening of the tips during a strip-and-pause retrieve.

Wings

The yarn is also well suited for supporting wing structures and adds breadth and color to the body, as featured in the Clark's Stonefly. This technique works equally well with streamer flies too.

Step 1: To form a foundation for the wing material, use 1 or 2 strands of combed yarn and secure tightly atop the hook. Do not exceed bend of hook.

Step 2: Tie in the wing material directly over the yarn. The final layer should also extend past the yarn. This foundation will also work

well for supporting marabou or arctic fox materials.

Technique #5: Body Wraps

The pliability of poly yarn makes it a very forgiving material to use. It is great for tying simple body configurations for dry or wet flies. You can vary the number of fibers to match relative fly size.

Basic Body Wrap

Step 1: Apply a thread base over the entire hook shank. Tie in the yarn at the front of the hook and cover it with thread wraps to the bend of the hook.

Step 2: Wrap the thread forward at a 45-degree angle to form a nice even taper on the body. If you desire a thicker body, use closer wraps of the yarn in each following turn.

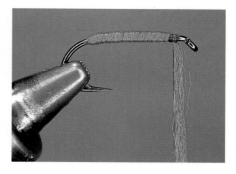

Step 3: Tie off the yarn at the front to complete the body. Note the even taper.

Forward Body Taper

It is very easy to change the shape of a body by forming an underbody first using the thread. The poly yarn will conform to the shape of the thread body as you wrap over it. This technique may be applied to body shapes on most adult aquatic insects.

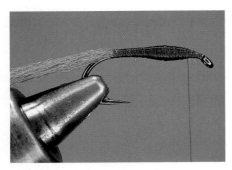

Step 1: Cover the hook with thread and tie in the yarn at the bend of the hook. Construct a body using layered thread wraps and build a forward taper.

Step 2: Wrap the yarn over the pre-formed body and tie off behind the eye.

Rear Body Taper

This body configuration may be applied to some terrestrial insects such as wasps, bees, or ants.

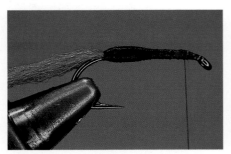

Step 1: Cover the hook with thread and tie in the yarn at the bend of the hook. Construct a body using layered thread wraps and build a rear taper at the back of the hook.

Step 2: Wrap the yarn over the pre-formed body and tie off behind the eye.

Twist 'n Wrap Body

Twisting the poly yarn before wrapping it around the hook adds bulk to the yarn and body, and gives some representation of a segmented body.

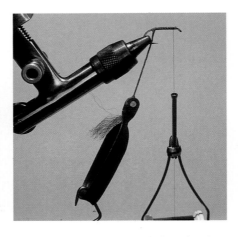

Step 1: Cover the hook with thread and tie in the yarn at the bend of the hook, return the thread to the front of the hook. Grasp the end of the yarn with English hackle pliers. Begin twisting the hackle pliers either by hand or with a hooked tool until the cord is fully twisted.

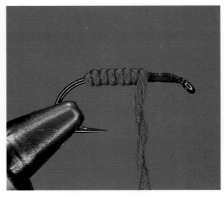

Step 2: Wrap the twisted cord around the hook shank and tie off.

Poly yarn has to be one of the easiest materials for wings and it is extremely buoyant. The latest bright colors also make it easier to see your fly on the water!

Wing Post

Wing posts are used for parachute type dry-fly patterns in which the hackle is wrapped around the base of the post. It appears parallel and flat to the fly's body instead of being wrapped around the hook shank. This style of dry-fly wing rides very well on top of the water's surface and has great visibility for the angler.

Step 1: Assuming the tail and body are complete, tie in a combed strand of yarn directly atop the hook; hold firmly and make tight thread wraps. Do not allow the yarn to slip to the sides of the hook shank. Don't be overly concerned about the forward length of yarn as you can always trim it later.

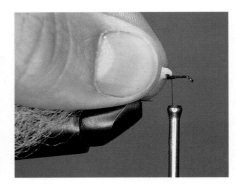

Step 2: Pull back on the wing and wrap the thread more than several times in front of the wing post. This will help guide the wing into a vertical position.

Step 3: Use several tight wraps of thread around the base of the post to complete the wing post. Add a drop or two of cement.

Step 4: The wing post completed. Trim the yarn off the back, cover with thread and tie in the hackle at the base of the post.

Fan-style and Split Wings

The following technique guides the tier through easy procedures to tie different styles of yarn wings from one series to the next. Whether you tie Compara-wings or spent wings, the poly yarn can do it all.

Fan-style Wing

The fan-style wing is often used for Compara-dun fly patterns. In most cases it is left hackleless so the silhouette of the fly's body and wing are unobstructed as it floats.

Step 1: Assuming the tail and body are complete, make a loop with a strand of yarn and tie directly atop the hook; hold firmly and make tight thread wraps.

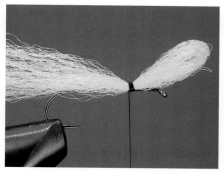

Step 2: The loop should extend over the front of the eye.

Step 3: Pull back on the loop and use several tight thread wraps in front of the loop.

Step 4: Cut the loop in half at the very top.

Step 5: Front view of cut loop. Notice how the yarn immediately takes to the shape of wings.

Step 6: Tease the yarn fibers apart and form the shape of a fan by using your fingers. Use several more wraps of thread behind and in front of the wing.

Step 7: Side view. Trim the yarn off the back, and cover with thread.

Split Vertical and Spent Wings

You can form divided wings from the fan-style wing or after you have cut the yarn loop.

Split Vertical Wings

Step 1: Front view of divided wings. Divide the yarn fibers as desired. Wrap the yarn in a figure-eight at the base of the yarn. Also include the thread wraps behind and in front of the yarn. For added strength use head cement on the thread wraps.

Spent Wings

This last procedure is another option if you were to change your mind about tying vertical wings and wanted to switch at the last minute to spent wings. Otherwise it would be faster and easier to lay a bundle of yarn across the top of the hook and make crisscross wraps over and around the yarn to form spent wings.

Step 1: Top view of spent wings. From the cut loop or fan-style wing position, pull and spread the yarn fibers into a flattened position forming the spent wings. Use crisscross thread wraps to hold the wings into position. Add head cement for extra strength.

Step 2: Front view of spent wings.

Technique #7: Twisted Yarn Body

When a strand of poly yarn is tightly stretched, twisted, and then folded in half and relaxed, it automatically curls up on itself forming a twisted helix-like cord. This has become a popular tying technique to shape bodies on many different types of dry flies. The twisted body has a very appealing conformation to match an insect's body and completes a very durable fly with great floatation.

Freehand Technique

Step 1: Hold the end of a yarn strand in one hand and with the other hand pull tightly on the free end of the yarn and begin twisting. Do not allow it to slip, keep tension on it at all times.

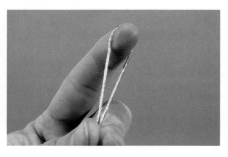

Step 2: Place the index finger of the hand doing the twisting under the middle of the yarn and raise the yarn upward into a loop.

Step 3: Quickly release the index finger from the loop to allow the yarn to twist itself into a spiral. If needed, twist the yarn in the same direction for a tighter twist.

Fastened Technique

Step 1: Firmly secure a strand of yarn on a hook where you want the body to be. Begin

to twist tightly on the yarn. Use your free hand to grasp the yarn in between each twist so it will not become unraveled.

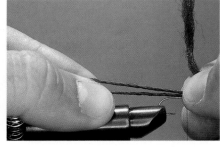

Step 2: Fold the twisted yarn in half and secure the tag end at the tie-in point of the body.

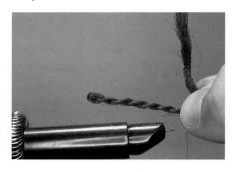

Step 3: Release the yarn to form the twisted body. If needed, twist the yarn to complete a tight spiral.

Step 4: Completed twisted body.

Technique #8: Yarn Shrouds

Lighter colored poly yarn veiled around other materials gives a transparent look when it is wet. It offers the realistic look of aquatic organisms such as insects and fish. Complete yarn shrouds tied off at both ends produce round to elongated bodies that can be coated with Soft Body plastic resin to make floating bugs. Bright underbodies are luminous through an enclosed yarn shroud, which is evident in the Sparkle Pupa caddis fly.

Caddis Yarn Shroud

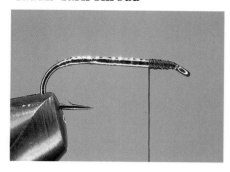

Step 1: Tie in a shiny or reflective type of material, such as tinsel or glass beads, to the hook.

Step 2: Use a sparse amount of combed yarn and lay it on the hook loosely. Roll the material around the hook as you wrap the thread around it.

Step 3: The yarn should surround the hook shank evenly.

Step 4: Trim the yarn at the front, and finish tying off the thread.

Streamer Yarn Shroud

Many baitfish patterns are marked with permanent markers. However, heavy barred grizzly will show through a thin shroud of light colored yarn and has a great baitfish look!

Step 1: Tie 3 to 4 heavy barred grizzly hackles on each side of the hook, with the dull sides facing inward.

Step 2: Use white or light cream poly yarn combed sparsely. Tie the yarn on each side of the hackles, covering them completely from top to bottom. The tips of the hackles should extend past the yarn.

Enclosed Yarn Shroud

This is an effective way to tie a transparent 3-D fly or simply form a large hollow body that will float well.

Step 1: Tie a thread foundation at the desired position where the rear of the shroud will be. Lay the yarn fibers over the hook and seat the yarn around the hook. Hold onto the yarn loosely and wrap the thread around the yarn, allowing the yarn to roll around the shank.

Step 2: Use several more tight wraps of thread to secure the yarn and advance the thread to the front of the hook.

Step 3: Spread out the yarn fibers at the rear of the hook so they are somewhat evenly dispersed around the hook.

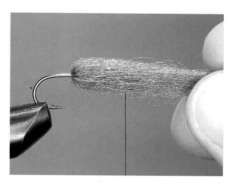

Step 4: Gather the yarn fibers and pull them forward to form an enclosed shroud.

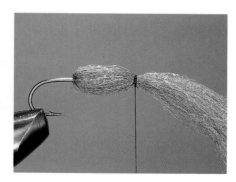

Step 5: Tie off the fibers with several loose wraps of thread.

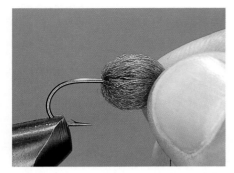

Step 6: You can adjust the roundness of the body by pushing or pulling against the yarn shroud. Note that pushing makes more of a sphere and pulling makes "less" of a sphere.

Step 7: Tie off the yarn tightly when you have the desired body shape. If there is enough material you can continue to form a wing. (Use this same technique for tying the Sparkle Caddis Pupa).

Technique #9: Spinning Yarn

Poly yarn can be spun like deer hair; the end result is a dense look which can be trimmed to the desired shape.

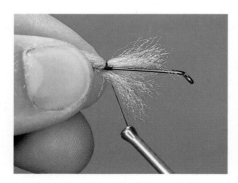

Step 1: Make a few wraps of thread on the hook for a foundation. Lay a bundle of yarn about 1 1/2 inches long over the thread. With a slightly loose grip on the yarn, wrap the thread around the yarn while during the

same movement allowing the thread to roll the yarn around the shank as shown. When you have completed the first wrap of thread around the yarn, let loose of the yarn. It should spin around the shank. Begin to make tighter thread wraps.

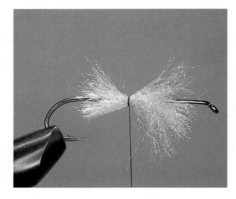

Step 2: The yarn should be evenly spun around the hook. Note the yarn is tied at its center.

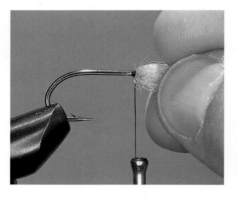

Step 3: Pull the yarn forward and bring the thread to the rear of the yarn. Make several tight thread wraps.

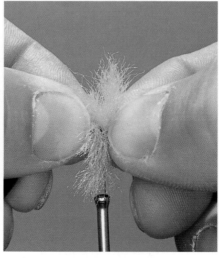

Step 4: Bring the thread to the front of the

yarn again. Use your thumb and index fingers to pack the yarn tightly.

Step 5: Add another bundle of yarn to the front and repeat Step 1 again, push and pack the yarn tightly against the preceding spun yarn.

Step 6: Repeat the process of spinning and packing until you have the desired amount of spun yarn on the hook.

Step 7: Completion of spun yarn.

Step 8: Trim the spun yarn to shape. Curved scissors are excellent for shaping the yarn.

Step 9: Use a permanent marker to make quick striations or markings. You can also spin two different colors of yarn.

Technique #10: Bundling Yarn

This particular tying technique is more prevalent in saltwater flies than fresh water. Although it is effective for tying freshwater imitations that bear thick bodies, such as dragonfly nymphs and crayfish. Yarn crab patterns are very popular in fly-fishing tropical saltwater flats where permit and bonefish thrive.

Step 1: Assuming the tail has been tied on, start with a small yarn bundle laid across the hook shank at its center. Criss-cross the thread tightly over the yarn.

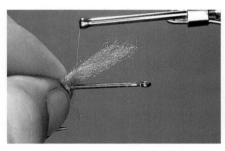

Step 2: Pull both sides of the first yarn bundle back and lay in the next color of yarn as close as possible and at a slight angle over the shank.

Step 3: Wrap the thread a couple of times over the second yarn bundle.

Step 4: Straighten the yarn bundle and begin to criss-cross the thread wraps back and forth over the yarn bundle. Make several tight wraps in front of the yarn bundle.

Step 5: Continue to alternate yarn colors until you have completed the body.

Step 6: Underside view.

Chapter Two
Wing-Style Body Dressing

WING-STYLE BODY DRESSING REFERS to flies in which the yarn is combed and tied atop the hook shank in a downwing fashion but actually serves as the body. This technique features several important attributes. Multiple colors can be mixed together easily, it's very simple and most important, the structure of the wing-style body is durable. Even though polypropylene floats, the material can still be applied to subsurface fly patterns. In fact, the poly yarn can be used to vary the sink rate by the density of the yarn and the amount of weight added to the

fly (e.g. lead-wrapped underbody, or beads).

Bob Long Jr., who ties most of his flies with synthetic materials, uses poly yarn for wings on his steelhead flies, which he says are fished close to the bottom. Examples of his work can be found at the end of this chapter. Poly yarn can also be used as an underwing material for dry flies or tied to represent the wing itself. As you scan the fly plates featuring wing-style body dressings, you will see there are no limitations to the type or size of fly one can tie using this technique.

Clark's Stonefly

Clark's Stonefly is one of the most widely accepted dry-fly patterns wherever stonefly hatches occur. Its home rivers are Oregon's Deschutes and the Metolius—two of the finest trout streams anywhere, where the fish and humbled anglers are many. A fly pattern that succeeds in fooling the older and keener rainbows from these two streams is a keeper. Clark's Stonefly has done so for nearly two decades!

Like the famed Woolly Bugger, the Clark's Stonefly requires little "well-heeled" tying experience to produce a quality fly that catches fish. We whole-heartedly agree with the quote from Mr. Kish on page 4.

Clark's Stonefly
Hook: 2X-long dry-fly hook, sizes 8-10
Thread: Orange 6/0
Body: Gold flat tinsel
Underwing: Rust and gold poly yarn, combed and mixed or straight orange
Wing: Deer hair
Hackle: Brown saddle

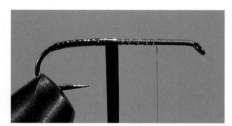

Step 1: Secure the thread behind the hook's eye and wrap the shank to the bend of the hook. Tie in a length of tinsel and bring the thread forward covering 2/3 of the hook. Wrap the tinsel over the thread until you reach the free end of the thread. Each wrap of tinsel should slightly overlap itself. Secure the tinsel tightly with the thread and trim tag end of tinsel.

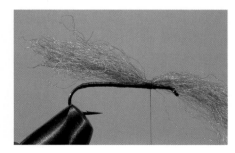

Step 2: Tie in the combed poly yarn fibers atop the hook. The end of the yarn fibers should not exceed more than 1/4 inch past

the bend of the hook. Trim the tag end at the front.

Step 3: Firmly secure a bundle of deer hair from the hide at the base of the fibers. Note the natural curve of the deer hair when you cut off the fibers. Do not stack the deer hair.

Step 4: Place the deer hair wing over the poly yarn with the curve of the tips sloping over and beyond the poly yarn about a 1/4 inch. To prevent flaring of the wing, use a light tension on the thread for the first few turns. Trim the butts of the hair down to a taper and continue wrapping with the tying thread to form a good base for the hackle.

Step 5: Tie in a saddle hackle and wrap three or four times at the front of the wing. Secure the hackle with the thread and whip-finish. Cut a V-notch at the bottom of the hackle to give the fly a lower profile as it sits on the water. Cement the head.
Note: The standard dry fly hackle is tied in with the dull side facing the tyer. I tie my hackle with the shiny side facing the tyer, to present a more life like silhouette and motion.

Clark's No Hackle Caddis
The Elk Hair Caddis is at the top of the list for adult caddis imitations. The standard is tied with a dubbed body, palmered hackle, and topped with an elk-hair wing. This version is much faster to tie because it has fewer tying steps. Three quick, easy steps and you're done. Thread, yarn, wing—and the fly is finished. You can tie them in yellow, brown, olive, and black, or if you want to match a body color more closely, simply mix a couple colors by combing them together.

Clark's No Hackle Caddis
Hook: Standard dry-fly hook, sizes 12-16
Thread: Tan 8/0
Body: Tan thread with tan poly yarn laid over top
Wing: Elk hair

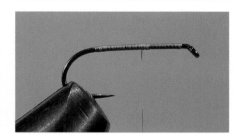

Step 1: Tie in the thread and cover the hook shank with tight wraps. Leave the thread at the tie in point for the yarn.

Step 2: Comb a strand of yarn until the fibers are opened and straight. Tie in the poly yarn

fibers atop the hook shank with the ends slightly past the bend of the hook.

Step 3: Secure the elk hair atop the yarn fibers, matching the hair's tips to the ends of the yarn fibers. Hold the hair with your thumb and index finger and use tight thread wraps around the elk hair causing the butts of the hair to flare out. Trim the elk hair to form a small head. Bring the thread to the front of the trimmed hair and wrap underneath. Whip-finish the thread to finish the fly.

Clark's Yarn Minnow

As a fly tier, I used to think that the more material I put on a hook, the better the fish could see it. I learned a big lesson a couple of years ago while fishing a desert lake in eastern Washington. The lake is known for its Lahontan cutthroat trout. In pods of three to eight fish, these fish cruise the shoreline well within fly-casting distance. Most of the time, a size 2 or 4 heavily dressed streamer was good enough to catch a fish or two, but after a while the fish became more leery of the fly. If the cast was accurate, I could get their attention quickly as I mimicked a fleeing minnow. However, there were many times when they would only follow the fly a short distance and then turn away.

The solution to this problem was to tie a sparse pattern using only half as much material on a smaller hook. From that fishing trip I learned that a suggestive pattern may only catch fish some of the time. Instead I was required to improve on the imitation by being more realistic or exact. Best of all, I was still able to use the poly yarn to perfect the pattern!

Clark's Yarn Minnow

Hook: 3X or 4X long streamer hook, sizes 4-8
Thread: Olive 6/0
Body: Silver flat Mylar tinsel
Wing: Gold and olive poly yarn or any color to match
Eyes: Painted, white with black pupil, enamel paint

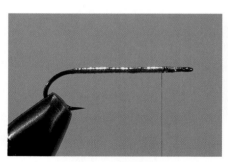

Step 1: Tie in thread and cover hook shank. At the bend of the hook, tie in a length of tinsel and return the thread to the front. Wrap the tinsel forward to the thread. Tie off the tinsel.

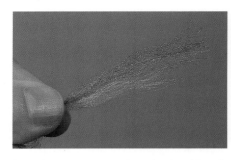

Step 2: Use one strand each of gold and olive poly yarn. Comb each strand of yarn separately until the fibers have opened up and are straight. Lay the olive strand of poly yarn over the gold strand and slightly extended past the tips.

Step 3: Mount the yarn wings about 2 lengths of the eye back from the hook eye. Use thread wraps to form an even, tapered head.

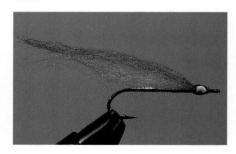

Step 4: Use the tip of a large quill or the head of pin and dip into white enamel paint to make an eye spot. Let it dry overnight and add a black pupil to the center of the white spot, use a smaller diameter point. When the paint is dry, apply head cement to the entire head and eyes.

Clark's Fluttering Stone
Hook: TMC 5212, sizes 6-12
Thread: Orange 6/0
Body: Gold tinsel
Underwing: Brown and gold Clark's Tying Yarn
Wing: Coastal deer hair
Hackle: 2 brown saddle hackles

Clark's Parachute Stone
Hook: TMC 5212, sizes 6-12
Thread: Orange 6/0
Body: Gold tinsel
Underwing: Orange Clark's Tying Yarn
Wing: Coastal deer hair
Hackle post: Fluorescent pink Clark's Tying Yarn
Hackle: 1 brown saddle hackle

Clark's Low Rider Stone
Hook: TMC 5212, sizes 6-12
Thread: Orange 6/0
Body: Gold tinsel
Underwing: Rust and gold Clark's Tying Yarn mixed
Hackle: 1 brown saddle hackle trimmed on top
Wing: Coastal deer hair
Head: Rust and gold Clark's Tying Yarn dubbed and formed with Soft Body

Clark's Stonefly
Tier: Mike Marchando
Hook: 3X long, curved, size 6
Thread: Black 6/0
Body: Gray, Clark's Tying Yarn palmered with dun hackle and trimmed
Underwing: Black, cream, and gray Clark's Tying Yarn mixed
Wing: Coastal deer hair
Hackle: 1 dun hackle

Clark's Stonefly
Tier: Mike Marchando
Hook: 2X long, size 10
Thread: Orange 6/0
Body: Gold tinsel
Underwing: Rust and gold Clark's Tying Yarn
Wing: Coastal deer hair
Hackle: Brown furnace

Clark's Stonefly
Tier: Charlie Boyce
Hook: 2X long, size 10
Thread: Orange 6/0
Body: Gold tinsel
Underwing: Orange Clark's Tying Yarn
Wing: Light elk hair
Hackle: Brown furnace hackle

Clark's Stonefly
Tier: Bill Myers
Hook: 2X long, size 10
Thread: Light olive 8/0
Body: Gold tinsel
Underwing: Gold and tan Clark's Tying Yarn
Wing: Elk hair
Hackle: Brown furnace hackle
Antennae: Elk hair

Clark's Stonefly
Tier: Bob Long Jr.
Hook: 2X long, size 8
Thread: Yellow 6/0
Body: Gold braid
Underwing: Gold Clark's Tying Yarn
Overwing: Elk hair
Hackle: Brown dyed grizzly hackle

Clark's Stonefly
Tier: Bob Long Jr.
Hook: 2X long, size 8
Thread: Red 6/0
Body: Gold braid
Underwing: Rust Clark's Tying Yarn
Wing: Elk hair
Hackle: Brown furnace hackle

Clark's Stonefly

Tier: Henry Hoffman
Hook: 2X long, size 6
Thread: Orange 6/0
Body: Gold tinsel
Underwing: Rust Clark's Tying Yarn
Wing: Coastal deer hair
Hackle: Brown Chickabou hackle tied parachute underneath

Clark's Stonefly

Tier: Gerry Clark
Hook: 2X long, size 10
Thread: yellow 6/0
Head: Deer hair shaped prior to other materials
Body: Gold tinsel
Underwing: Rust and gold Clark's Tying Yarn
Wing: Coastal deer hair
Hackle: Brown

Clark's Stonefly

Tier: Ken Taylor
Hook: 2X long, size 8
Thread: Orange 6/0
Body: Orange poly yarn
Underwing: Orange Clark's Tying Yarn
Wing: Coastal deer hair
Hackle: Brown furnace hackle
Antennae: Stripped hackle stem

Clark's Stonefly

Tier: Henry Hoffman
Hook: 2X long, size 8
Thread: Orange 6/0
Body: Gold tinsel
Underwing: Gold Clark's Tying Yarn
Wing: Coastal deer hair
Hackle: Brown hackle tied parachute underneath

Clark's Stonefly

Tier: Gerry Clark
Hook: 2X long, 10
Thread: Yellow 6/0
Body: Gold tinsel
Underwing: Gold and rust Clark's Tying Yarn
Wing: Coastal deer hair
Hackle: Orange, black, and brown Clark's Tying Yarn

Little Yellow Stone

Tier: Alan Cline
Hook: Dry fly, sizes 12 and 14
Thread: Yellow 6/0
Body: Holographic Mylar
Underwing: Gold Clark's Tying Yarn
Wing: Light elk hair
Hackle: White

Clark's Stonefly

Tier: Chuck Cameron
Hook: 3X long, curved, size 6
Thread: Orange 6/0
Body: Gold tinsel
Underwing: Orange Clark's Tying Yarn
Thorax: Rust Clark's Tying Yarn
Wing: Elk hair
Hackle: Brown

Clark's Stonefly

Tier: Chris Mihulka
Hook: 2X long, size 8
Thread: Black 6/0
Body: Orange Clark's Tying Yarn
Underwing: Yellow and orange Clark's Tying Yarn
Wing: Light elk hair
Thorax: Gold floss
Hackle: Brown furnace hackle

Clark's Salmon Fly

Hook: 2X long, size 8
Thread: Orange 6/0
Body: copper tinsel
Underwing: Rust Clark's Tying Yarn
Wing: Black dyed deer hair
Hackle: Brown furnace hackle

Clark's Salmon Fly

Tier: Gerry Clark

Hook: Daiichi 2340, size 8

Thread: Flame 6/0

Body: Gold tinsel

Underwing: Orange Clark's Tying Yarn

Wing: Coastal deer hair

Head and collar: Deer hair tied reversed to form a bullet head

Clark's Deer Hair Caddis, Olive

Hook: TMC 5212, sizes 14-18

Thread: Olive 6/0

Body: Gold tinsel

Underwing: Olive and black Clark's Tying Yarn mixed

Overwing: Coastal deer hair

Hackle: 1 olive dyed grizzly hackle

Clark's Deer Hair Caddis, Black

Hook: 2X long, sizes 14-18

Thread: Black 6/0

Body: Gold tinsel

Underwing: Black Clark's Tying Yarn mixed

Overwing: Coastal deer hair

Hackle: Black

McKenzie Caddis

Tier: Alan Cline

Hook: 2X long, size 10

Thread: Light olive 6/0

Body: Holographic Mylar

Underwing: Fluorescent green Clark's Tying Yarn

Wing: Mixture of Whitlock's blue and dun deer to imitate a fluttering caddis

Hackle: Dun

Little Green Caddis

Tier: Bill Myers

Hook: Dry fly, size 14

Thread: Light olive

Body: Tying thread

Underwing: Light olive and gold Clark's Tying Yarn

Wing: Coastal deer hair

Hackle: Olive

Antennae: Hackle stem

Clark's Hair Caddis, Tan

Originator and tier: Bob Long Jr.

Hook: 3X long, size 8

Thread: Brown 6/0

Body: Metallic green Sparkle Braid

Rib: Dark brown

Wing: Tan Clark's Tying Yarn

Clark's Hair Caddis, Black

Originator and tier: Bob Long Jr.

Hook: 3X long, size 8

Thread: Black 6/0

Body: Copper Sparkle Braid

Rib: Dark brown

Wing: Black Clark's Tying Yarn

Yarn Caddis

Originator and tier: Bob Long Jr.

Hook: TMC 900BL, #10

Thread: Yellow 6/0

Body: Olive poly dubbing

Rib: White dry-fly hackle

Wing: 8 strands of pearl Krystal Flash and white Clark's Tying Yarn

Steelhead Caddis, White

Originator and tier: Bob Long Jr.

Hook: 3X long, size 8

Thread: Brown 6/0

Body: Tan poly dubbing

Rib: Light brown hackle

Wing: 6 strands of pearl Mylar and white Clark's Tying Yarn

Drifting Steelhead Caddis

Originator and tier: Bob Long Jr.

Hook: TMC 200, Mustad 80050, Dai-Riki 270

Thread: Flame orange 6/0

Tail: Orange Clark's Tying Yarn

Body: Sparkle Chenille

Rib: White saddle hackle

Wing: Yellow and orange Clark's Tying Yarn

BossBob's Damsel Fly

Originator and tier: Bob Long Jr.

Hook: Dry fly, #10

Thread: Yellow 6/0

Tail: 1/16 Live Body closed-cell foam

Back: Yellow or olive Nymph Back

Body: Sparkle Chenille

Rib: White saddle hackle

Wing: White Clark's Tying Yarn

Legs: 6 strands of Krystal Flash

Eyes: Olive Umpqua mono eyes, ex. small

Young of the Year Minnow (dace)

Originator and tier: Bob Long Jr.

Hook: Short, size 6

Thread: Black 6/0

Tail: Tuft of filoplume

Body: 6 wraps of .020" lead wire

Belly: White poly yarn

Top: 6 strands of Krystal Flash and other flashes or tinsels, doubled over on itself to make 12 strands

Wing: Olive poly yarn

Collar: Bright red thread

Eyes: Gold bead chain

Young of the Year Minnow (shiner)

Originator and tier: Bob Long Jr.

Hook: Short, 6 size

Thread: Bright red 6/0

Tail: Tuft of filoplume

Body: 6 wraps of .020" lead wire

Belly: Bright orange poly yarn

Top: 6 strands of Krystal Flash and other flashes or tinsels, doubled over on itself to make 12 strands

Wing: Light brown poly yarn

Eyes: Gold bead chain

Young of the Year Minnow (bluegill)

Originator and tier: Bob Long Jr.

Hook: Short, size 6

Thread: Bright red 6/0

Tail: Tuft of filoplume

Body: 6 wraps of .020" lead wire

Belly: Bright yellow poly yarn then a touch of bright orange poly yarn

Top: 6 strands of Krystal Flash and other flashes or tinsels, doubled over on itself to make 12 strands

Wing: Olive poly yarn, a brown marker is used to color the front edge of the wing

Eyes: Gold bead chain

Lil' Darlin' Minnow, white

Originator and tier: Bob Long Jr.

Hook: Wet fly, size 8

Thread: Black 6/0

Body: 6 wraps of .20" lead wire and the tail portion of a Mr. Twister Sassy Shiner, color to match the wing, size small

Wing: White Clark's Tying Yarn and pearl Krystal Flash or similar flashing material

Eyes: Silver bead chain

Note: The tail portion of the Mr. Twister Sassy Shiner is attached by heating the hook before trying to penetrate the plastic.

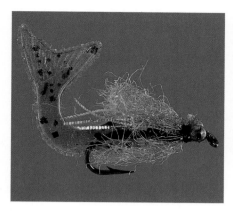

Lil' Darlin' Minnow

Originator and tier: Bob Long Jr.

Hook: Wet fly, size 8

Thread: Brown 6/0

Body: 6 wraps of .20" lead wire and the tail portion of a Mr. Twister Sassy Shiner, color to match the wing, size small

Wing: Light brown Clark's Tying Yarn and pearl Krystal Flash or similar flashing material

Eyes: Gold bead chain

Clark's Bluegill Special

Hook: 2X long, size 10

Thread: Black 6/0

Tail: Red hackle fibers

Body: Silver tinsel

Underwing: Light purple polypropylene yarn

Hackle: Partridge feather

Wing: Purple dyed gray squirrel tail

Muddler Minnow

Tier: Aaron Ostoj

Hook: 3X long, size 4

Thread: Orange 6/0

Tail: Red squirrel tail

Body: Gold tinsel

Rib: Brown hackle, trimmed

Underwing: Orange Clark's Tying Yarn

Wing: Red squirrel tail

Head and collar: Natural deer body hair, spun and trimmed as shown

Pearl Yeti

Originator and tier: Ken Hanley

Hook: Salmon/steelhead, light wire, sizes 4-1/0

Thread: Black or white 8/0

Tag: Fluorescent green floss

Butt: Silver tinsel thread

Tail: White polypropylene yarn

Body: Lite Brite, pearl blue

Wing: White bucktail

Collar: Natural teal flank feather

Mary's Pond Purple

Hook: 2X long, size 10

Thread: Black 6/0

Body: Silver tinsel

Underwing: Light purple polypropylene yarn and 8 peacock sword fibers

Wing: Mallard fibers

Hackle: Black saddle hackle

Synthetic Bead Head Streamer (silver and white)

Originator and tier: Bob Long Jr.

Hook: 3X long, curved, size 6

Thread: Red 6/0

Head: Brass or copper bead

Belly: Pearl Sparkle Flash

Top: White poly yarn, then silver Sparkle Flash

Synthetic Bead Head Streamer (chartreuse and white)

Originator and tier: Bob Long Jr.

Hook: 3X long, curved, size 6

Thread: Red 6/0

Head: Brass or copper bead

Belly: Pearl Sparkle Flash

Top: White poly yarn, then chartreuse Sparkle Flash

Synthetic Bead Head Streamer (Olive and gold)
Originator and tier: Bob Long Jr.
Hook: 3 X long, curved, size 6
Thread: Red 6/0
Head: Brass or copper bead
Belly: Pearl Sparkle Flash
Top: Gold poly yarn, then light olive Sparkle Flash

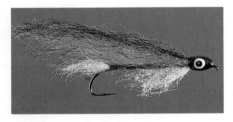

Clark's Poly Red Side Shiner
Hook: 6X long, size 4-8
Thread: Olive 6/0
Tail: White polypropylene yarn
Body: A thin strip cut from a Frito-Lay chip bag
Overbody: A sparse bunch of combed polypropylene yarn; gold or tan topped with a mix of black and olive
Throat: White polypropylene yarn
Eyes: Black and white enamel paint

Yarn Clouser
Tier: Bob Long Jr.
Hook: Mustad 92553R, size 2
Thread: Red 3/0
Body: Black polypropylene yarn, 8 strands of Krystal Flash, white polypropylene yarn, and brown polypropylene yarn
Eyes: Dumbbell

Poly Bear Bluegill
Originator and tier: Greg Webster
Hook: Saltwater or bass hook, size 2
Thread: Clear mono
Wing: Baitfish color Angel Hair over baitfish color Poly Bear over sky blue Poly Bear
Bottom: Orange Poly Bear over yellow Poly Bear
Side wing: Tie baitfish color Poly Bear sparsely over sky blue portion of top wing (both sides)
Eyes: Red epoxy Prismatic Eyes
Markings: Permanent marker, blue ear (both sides), black vertical markings over baitfish and sky blue Poly Bear
Head: 2 or 3 coats of Angler's Choice Soft Body (first coat should be with the thin mixture)

Ed's Redfish Special
Originator and tier: Ed Rizzolo
Hook: Standard salt water, size 4
Thread: Black 6/0
Tail: Orange Clark's Tying Yarn
Body: Gold tinsel overwrapped with Larva Lace
Eyes: Silver bead chain
Belly: Orange then a few fibers of black Clark's Tying Yarn
Cheek: 1 natural grizzly hackle on each side
Beard: 8 strands gold Krystal Flash

Poly Bear Streamer, Shad
Originator and tier: Greg Webster
Hook: Saltwater or bass hook
Thread: Clear mono or white 3/0
Top Wing: White Poly Bear over baitfish color Angel Hair over white Poly Bear
Bottom: White Poly Bear
Throat: Red Poly Bear
Side Wing: Gray Poly Bear tied sparsely over the center of the body on both sides
Eyes: Silver prismatic epoxy eyes
Head: 2 or 3 coats of Anglers Choice Soft Body (first coat should be with the thin mixture)

Kootenay Lake Streamer, black and white
Tier: Chuck Brunham
Hook: 1/0 standard saltwater, 1/0 octopus bait hook for the trailer
Thread: Black 3/0
Body: Pearl Mylar tubing, medium
Wing: White Clark's Tying Yarn, white polar bear, holographic Mylar Motion, gold and silver Krystal Flash, black bucktail, and on the top, black Clark's Tying Yarn
Eyes: Prismatic, small

Kootenay Lake Streamer, green

Tier: Chuck Brunham

Hook: 1/0 standard salt water, 1/0 octopus bait hook for the trailer

Thread: Black 3/0

Body: Olive chenille

Rib: Gold wire

Wing: Black and olive Clark's Tying Yarn mixed, each side is placed a small bundle of pearl Krystal Flash, then completed with green dyed bucktail

Eyes: Prismatic, small

Orange Yarn Spey Fly

Tier: Aaron Ostoj

Hook: Standard salmon fly hook

Thread: Fluorescent red 6/0

Tail: Orange and red Clark's Tying Yarn mixed with orange Krystal Flash

Body: Orange seal or Angora dubbing

Sides: Jungle cock along side of rear wing

Rear Wing: Orange and red Clark's Tying Yarn mixed with orange Krystal Flash

Hackle: Three turns of orange marabou, followed by two turns of golden pheasant breast

Front Wing: Orange and red Clark's Tying Yarn mixed with orange Krystal Flash

Poly Shrimp

Tier: Aaron Ostoj

Hook: Alec Jackson Spey, sizes 5-1 1/2 or equivalent

Weight: 10-20 turns of fine lead wire

Thread: Fluorescent red 6/0

Body: Orange and pink Angora or seal

Hackle: Webbed brown hen over 1/3 of body

Shellback: Orange and fluorescent pink Clark's Tying Yarn and orange Krystal Flash

Clark's Wiggler

Tier: Bob Long Jr.

Hook: TMC 200

Thread: Black 6/0

Tail: Yellow Clark's Tying Yarn

Body: Red Chenille

Legs: Red hackle palmered

Shellback: Yellow Clark's Tying Yarn

Rib: Heavy black thread

Poly Yarn Practitioner

Tier: Aaron Ostoj

Hook: Standard salmon fly hook

Thread: Orange 6/0

Tail: Orange Clark's Tying Yarn

Body: Orange wool yarn

Antennae: Golden pheasant tippet

Hackle: Orange saddle

Wing: Orange Clark's Tying Yarn

Jock Scott

Tier: Aaron Ostoj

Hook: Alec Jackson Spey Hook, 1 1/2

Thread: Black 8/0

Tip: Fine oval silver tinsel

Tag: Yellow Clark's Tying Yarn, wrapped as floss

Tail: Golden pheasant crest and orange Clark's Tying Yarn

Butt: Black ostrich herl

Body: Rear half, yellow Clark's Tying Yarn wrapped as floss; veiled above and below with same, butted with black ostrich herl; front half, black Clark's Tying Yarn wrapped as floss

Ribbing: Oval silver tinsel over both halves of body

Hackle: Black saddle over front half only

Throat: Speckled guinea

Wing: Clark's Tying Yarn layered in the following order: black mixed with orange, blue, yellow, red, and black mixed with orange

Cheeks: Jungle cock

Sides: Kingfisher

Topping: Golden pheasant crest

Chapter Three
Yarn-Wrap Body Dressings

THERE ARE NUMEROUS WAYS FOR fly-tying materials to be wrapped around a hook. But stop and think about how many different types of materials you might use for the many ways of dressing a fly in a 3-dimensional 360-degree fashion. If you have already covered Chapter One in this book then you know that poly yarn can be dressed around a hook in various ways. This chapter will present three tying methods (and effective trout patterns) for easy tying, keeping in mind the last-minute fly tier/fisher who always seems to wait until the night before their fishing trip to fill their fly boxes!

Clark's No Hackle PMD

When I tie flies, most of the time my main objective is to tie them quickly with limited materials. The Pale Morning Dun is a good example. A tail, wrapped body, and a wing, all made from poly yarn. Simple, don't you think? Obviously, this approach can be applied to any mayfly pattern. I have used this pattern for pale morning dun hatches on the Fall and Metolius rivers.

Clark's No Hackle PMD
Hook: Standard dry-fly hook, sizes 16-18
Thread: Olive 8/0
Tail: A minute amount of white poly yarn
Body: Gold and olive poly yarn combed together
Wing: Cream poly yarn

Step 1: Cover the hook shank with thread. Tie in the tail just before the bend of the hook. Trim excess yarn.

Step 2: Tie in the body yarn atop the hook and slightly back from the eye. Completely wrap over the yarn to where the tail begins.

Step 3: Wrap the thread to the front again and shape a forward taper to create the thorax.

Step 4: Wrap the body yarn forward over the thread wraps. You should notice a taper to the body and thorax.

Step 5: Tie in a small bundle of wing material over the top of thorax area and slightly back from the eye (leave plenty of room to finish the thread). Before securing the thread tightly, rearrange the wing material into a fan

shape. Make several more tight thread wraps.

Step 6: Trim the hind fibers from the wing material and finish with ample thread wraps. Move the thread to the front of the wing material. Make enough tight thread wraps to support the wing in an upright posture. Whip-finish the thread to complete the fly.

Clark's Flying Ant

How popular are ant patterns? For every fly pattern book there's a varied ant imitation. Each one features a different tying style with its own body material e.g., closed-cell foam, dubbing of all sorts, and even tying thread. Each material takes time and patience to achieve the ant's unique body silhouette. The body of this adult ant pattern is fashioned simply with poly yarn, and because the strand is twisted and then wrapped around the hook, the bulk of the body is built quickly. The shape of the ant's head is perfected with a quick snip of the scissors!

Clark's Flying Ant
Hook: Standard dry-fly hook, sizes 10-14
Thread: Black 8/0
Body: Black poly yarn
Wing: Gray poly yarn
Legs: Black neck hackle

Step 1: Cover the hook shank with thread. At the rear of the hook tie in the yarn for the body atop the hook with about 1/2 inch of yarn extending past the front and 3" past the bend. Completely wrap the thread over the body yarn to the front.

Step 2: Trim the yarn extended over the front close to the eye leaving a tuft of yarn to form the head. Grasp the body yarn and twist into a tight cord. Wrap the twisted yarn over 2/3 of hook and tie it off.

Step 3: Tie in the wing material and secure tightly.

Step 4: Tie in a black hackle and make 3-4 wraps. Tie it off tightly with thread. Whip-finish the thread in front of the yarn tuft to complete the fly.

Poly-wag Dog Nymph

Dubbing materials are often used to create a "buggy" look. Naturally, I had to try using my poly yarn as a dubbing material. I hacked it into little pieces after the usual combing. The initial attempt was horrible; being what plastic is, its slick finish wouldn't even adhere to a well-waxed tying thread. It needed substance. I happened to look down at Katy, my gold cocker spaniel, and immediately found my source. I realized her hair could be used as a binder for the slick poly yarn. Katy lifted her relaxed head from her paws as I smiled at her. She's always with me at my tying desk, and somehow I sensed she knew what I was about to do. She started wagging her tail and held still for me as I raked my tying comb through her curly, golden fur to collect some of the shedding hair. Then I mixed the natural hair with the small cut pieces of poly yarn together by hand. With the thread-core direct dubbing technique I was now able to achieve a dubbed body.

For those of you who are not pet owners, any natural underfur, such as rabbit, fox, or muskrat will do the trick. A blender is also highly recommended for mixing as described in Technique #2, page 9.

Poly-wag Dog Nymph

Hook: 1X long nymph hook, sizes 12-16
Thread: Tan 8/0
Tail: Partridge fibers
Ribbing: Fine copper or gold wire
Body: Black, light brown, and sand poly yarn blended with supple animal fur; 50:50
Wingcase: Black and sand yarn strip formed and hardened with Soft Body plastic resin
Thorax: Same as body

Step 1: Cover the hook shank with thread. At the bend of the hook, tie in partridge fibers for the tail; about half of the length hook shank. Tie in the wire ribbing.

Step 2: With pre-mixed poly dubbing (Technique #2), use the thread-core direct dubbing method and form a tapered body.

Step 3: Wrap the wire forward in moderate spacing to form the ribbing. For the wing-case, tie in a thin strip of yarn coated with Soft Body.

Step 4: Apply direct dubbing to thread and form the thorax slightly larger than the body. Pull the wingcase over the thorax and tie it off. Trim excess wingcase and whip-finish the thread to complete the fly.

BossBob's Larva Lace

Originator and tier: Bob Long Jr.
Hook: TMC 200
Thread: Brown 6/0
Tail: Moose mane
Underbody: Flat, wide, gold tinsel
Body: Yellow lace
Case: Turkey
Thorax: Clark's Tying Yarn dubbed and picked out
Antennae: Moose mane

Soft Hackle Stone Nymph

Originator and tier: Henry Hoffman
Hook: Mustad 9672, size 6
Thread: Brown 3/0, rear; orange 6/0, front
Tail: Brown chicken biot
Weight: 2 strands of .025 lead wire twisted into a rope, one piece lashed onto each side of hook
Abdomen: Brown Clark's Tying Yarn
Thorax: Rust Clark's Tying Yarn
Hackle: Barred brown soft-hackle flank feather, trimmed off on right side then palmered over the thorax
Antennae: Brown chicken biot
Eyes: Spirit River black mono

Dunham's Stonefly

Originator and tier: Duane Dunham
Hook: 2X long, sizes 6-10
Thread: Orange 6/0
Tail: Elk hair
Body: Gold polypropylene yarn twisted then wrapped around shaft to show a segmented body
Wing: Elk hair
Hackle post: Elk hair
Hackle: 1 light brown hackle

Clark's Skirted Caddis

Hook: Standard wet, sizes 12-16
Thread: Black 6/0
Body: Gold tinsel and orange Clark's Tying Yarn
Collar: Partridge
Head: Peacock herl

Wrapped, Twisted Body Caddis

Tier: Lee Clark
Hook: Standard wet, sizes 12-16
Thread: Black 6/0
Body: Cream Clark's Tying Yarn
Head: Black Clark's Tying Yarn

Gerry's Scud

Tier: Gerry Clark
Hook: Traditional nymph, size 12 to 16
Thread: Orange 6/0
Body: Orange and gold mixed, Clark's Tying Yarn dubbed
Note: The dubbed body is brushed after the fly is completed.

Gerry's Caddis Pupa

Tier: Gerry Clark
Hook: Traditional nymph, size 12
Thread: Black 6/0
Body: Rust, gold, and orange Clark's Tying Yarn dubbed then trimmed
Collar: Black Clark's Tying Yarn dubbed

Green Rock Worm

Tier: Lee Clark
Hook: Standard wet, sizes 12-16
Thread: Black 6/0
Body: Tan, green, brown, and black Clark's Tying Yarn mixed and dubbed
Rib: Fine gold wire
Head: Black and green Clark's Tying Yarn mixed and dubbed

Bill's Dragonfly Nymph

Originator and tier: Bill Myers
Hook: Standard wet, 2X long size 6
Thread: Olive 8/0
Body: Olive Clark's Tying Yarn
Legs: Olive Clark's Tying Yarn
Eyes: Green mono
Head: Olive Clark's Tying Yarn

Yarn and Chickabou Dragonfly Nymph

Originator and tier: Henry Hoffman
Hook: Dai-Riki 710, size 6 or 8
Thread: Olive 6/0 olive dun
Tail: Barred olive Chickabou plume
Weight: 2 strands of .025 lead wire twisted into rope, one piece lashed onto each side of hook
Body: Olive Clark's Tying Yarn
Hackle: Section of rooster barred olive soft hackle
Wingcase: Lacquered rooster barred olive soft-hackle tip v-notched
Eyes: Mono

Chapter 4
Twisted-Yarn Body Dressing

THE TWISTED-BODY TECHNIQUE CAME accidentally one day from one of my high school students. It was my preparation period and I was in the process of clearing off my desk. All that remained were a couple colored pencils, an old dictionary, and some short pieces of poly yarn. Brad Weigandt strolled into my classroom as he often did just to talk. He had a habit of always picking up something off my desk and playing with it. This time it just happened to be a strand of yarn, but I wasn't aware of what he was doing with it until the bell rang to end the period. He quickly dropped the

yarn on my desk and said, "See you later," and out the door he sped. I looked at my desk to notice that the strand of yarn Brad was playing with was now very different—it was spiraled instead of a loose strand. Wow! I thought to myself. What a great idea for fly tying! Guess what I did as soon as I returned home?

The first pattern I tied using this technique was the Twisted Body Clark's Stonefly. Later, I applied the technique to the mayfly, caddisfly, damselfly, and a grasshopper pattern. The key to this method is using the proper number of filaments for the size of fly you imitate.

See Chapter 1, Technique #7, page 14.

Clark's Big Yellow Mayfly
Each year about the middle of July, the big yellow mayflies (*Hexagenia*) hatch at one of my favorite lakes. The emergence of these large bugs typically begins shortly before dark if the day is warm and sunny. To match the hatch, I tied my first Yellow Mayfly patterns using the extended deer-hair body, parachute pattern. It worked quite well, but it needed to be replaced after every fifth or sixth fish, because the trout literally destroyed the deer-hair body.

Once the twisting technique was discovered I immediately switched to using the poly yarn for a more durable fly. However, this was not the main reason I started using poly yarn. The improved fly was designed for my wife, Betty, who fished flies using a spinning rod with a bubble. To fish the fly effectively with this outfit, the fly had to be durable, buoyant, and balanced enough to land right side up after a cast. The fly was rigged with 3 1/2 feet of leader below a clear plastic bubble. I have personally used this pattern for several years and have found it to land right-side-up most of the time and to ride naturally on the water, especially in rough weather conditions. It just doesn't tip over.

Clark's Big Yellow Mayfly

Hook: 2X long, 1X fine dry-fly hook, size 10

Thread: Yellow 6/0

Body: Gold Mylar and yellow poly yarn, one strand

Wing post: Yellow poly yarn

Hackle: Chartreuse or yellow dyed grizzly

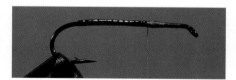

Step 1: Cover the hook shank with thread from the front to the bend. Tie in the gold tinsel and wrap forward covering about 2/3 of the hook shank.

Step 2: Cut three 4" strands of poly yarn.

Comb together and twist. Tie in the twisted yarn body atop the hook shank with the body extending past the bend about half of the shank length. Trim the excess yarn at the front.

Step 3: Tie in a strand of yarn for the wing post atop the tie-in point of body. Once the wing-post material is secured around the body, trim excess material. Advance the thread to the front of the wing post and make tight wraps around the hook and close to the base of the wing post. To complete the wing post make several more wraps of the thread around its base.

Step 4: Tie in the hackle at the base of the wing post and secure the stem of the hackle at an oblique angle ahead of the wing post. The hackle will be tied off with the thread at the same point.

Step 5: Wrap the hackle 4-5 times around the base of the wing post keeping it close to the base of the post. Tie off the hackle and whip-finish the thread of the fly to complete.

Clark's Damselfly

After designing the Big Yellow Mayfly I thought about other fly patterns I could tie using the twisting technique. Other adult insects with long, narrow bodies came to mind; caddisflies, grasshoppers,

dragonflies, and damselflies. I just happened to have a nice color of damsel blue poly yarn so I began to study the major characteristics and shape of the real insect. The following summer, I was at one of my favorite trout lakes ready to test my new damselfly. While sitting in my boat about forty feet from shore, I observed something I had never seen before. Around six damselflies, like a squadron of war planes, were flying inches above the water. Then I heard a couple of splashes from fish feeding off the surface. It didn't appear they were rising to damselflies but I decided to try my new pattern anyway. I placed my cast in the vicinity of the rising fish. Crash! A small rainbow took it. What a thrill in dry-fly fishing. There is nothing more exciting than to go through the process of creating your own fly pattern and being rewarded with the sight of a rising fish taking your imitation!

Clark's Damselfly

Hook: 2X long, 1X fine, size 10

Thread: Blue 6/0

Body: Light blue Mylar or polypropylene strip and blue poly yarn

Wing: Dark bucktail or deer hair

Hackle: Dark saddle

Wingcase: Blue poly yarn from body

Head: Same as wingcase

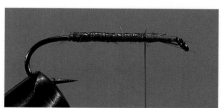

Step 1: Cover the hook shank with thread from the front to the bend. Tie in the blue Mylar strip and cover about 2/3 of the hook shank.

Step 2: Cut one 4" strand of poly yarn and twist. Tie in the twisted yarn body atop the hook shank extending at least the full length of the shank past the bend of the hook. Be sure to leave plenty of yarn out the front for the wingcase and head.

Step 3: Tie in a sparse amount of bucktail over the body but do not exceed its length.

Step 4: Make a few more thread wraps over the yarn to within one eye length of the hook eye. Pull the yarn back over the wing and wrap the thread over the yarn. Tie in the hackle and continue to wrap the thread to just short of the hook eye.

Step 5: Wrap the hackle 3-4 turns and tie off with the thread. Pull the yarn over the middle of the hackle to form the wingcase and tie off with a whip-finish. Trim the yarn about 1/8 inch above hook eye.

Clark's Blue-Winged Olive Dun

The Blue-Winged Olive mayfly is a good example of following an important fly-tying principle, not to overdress small flies. The size of the hook dictates the quantity of material to use. A couple dozen or less filaments may be all it takes for body. Once again the virtue of poly yarn even caters to miniature patterns for effective imitation and great buoyancy.

Clark's Blue-Winged Olive Dun
Hook: Standard dry-fly hook, sizes 14-16
Thread: Light olive, 8/0
Body: Olive poly yarn
Wing: White poly yarn
Hackle: Olive dun or olive dyed grizzly
Tail: Olive thread, 8/0

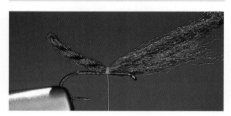

Step 1: Cover the first 1/3 of the hook with a thread base. Cut one 4" yarn strand and comb it out seperating the filaments. Use about 1/4 of them to form a twisted body. Tie on the extended, twisted body so it extends slightly past the bend of the hook.

Step 2: Tie in a thin strand of poly yarn for the wing just ahead of the body. Note that tying the wing for the Blue-Winged Olive is similar to the Big Yellow Mayfly but with the option of securing the wing from the front

instead of the back. Both tying techniques accomplish the same task of forming the wing post giving the tier either option to be comfortable with.

Step 3: Tie in the hackle at the base and ahead of the wing post.

Step 4: Wrap the hackle 4-5 times around the base of the wing post. Tie it off and whip-finish the thread to complete.

Step 5: Trim wing post to desired height.

Step 6: For the tail appendages, cut a piece of tying thread about 4-5 inches long. Thread a sewing needle and make certain the tag ends are offset from each other. Insert the needle at the tip of the body and draw thread through it until the first tag end of the thread comes out. Remove the sewing needle.

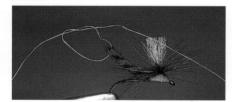

Step 7: Pull the thread through the body until you have an even length of both tag ends. Make an overhand knot and draw it tight to the body. Repeat the process a

second time. Trim the tag ends to the desired length to complete the tail.

Step 8: Don't be overly concerned about the tail fibers not being straight as catching performance is not hindered. However, if you're a perfectionist, stroke some head cement or Soft Body over the thread to straighten.
Note: this thread tail technique was devised by Bill Myers of Prineville, Oregon.

Clark's Twisted Body Stone
Hook: 2X long, sizes 6-12
Thread: Orange 6/0
Body: Gold tinsel
Underwing: Orange poly yarn, twisted
Overwing: Coastal deer hair
Hackle: 1 brown saddle hackle

Extended Body Caddis
Tier: Bill Myers
Hook: Standard dry, sizes 16 and 18
Thread: Olive 8/0
Hackle: Olive
Body: Olive Clark's Tying Yarn
Wing: Dark mottled turkey, V-notched, tied tent style
Antennae: Stripped stem of an olive hackle

Clark's Green Drake Parachute
Hook: Standard dry, 2X long, size 12
Thread: Olive 6/0
Body: Olive Clark's Tying Yarn
Wing: Gray Clark's Tying Yarn
Hackle: Olive

Organza Damsel Adult
Originator and tier: Keith Burkhart
Hook: TMC 100, size 8
Thread: White 8/0
Body: Fine & Dry Damsel Blue in front, then blue Clark's Tying Yarn with blue Krystal Flash
Wing: Organza filaments
Hackle: Grizzly

Adult Damsel
Tier: Ed Rizzolo
Hook: Standard dry, 3X long, size 12
Thread: White 8/0
Body: Blue Clark's Tying Yarn, and black permanent marker
Wingcase and hackle post: A loop of blue Clark's Tying Yarn
Wing: Grizzly tied parachute style
Head: White thread
Eyes: Burnt monofilament

Mr. XX
Originator & Tier: Chris Mihulka
Hook: 2X long, size 6-10
Thread: Orange 6/0
Body: Orange polypropylene yarn twisted
Wing: Natural deer hair
Head and collar: Orange brown dyed deer hair tied reversed to form a bullet head; the collar should be trimmed on the bottom
Legs: Orange rubber hackle, 2 tied on each side

Dragon's Tooth
Originator and tier: Ken Hanley
Hook: Saltwater style, sizes 4-6
Thread: Red or black 8/0
Tail: Red Clark's Tying Yarn twisted
Body; 1st half: Angora goat, dark red (claret), apply a few wraps with a dubbing loop
Wing/Legs: Spandex or rubber hackle, white, exaggerate the length
Body; 2nd half: Angora goat, dark red (claret), use a dubbing loop
Head: Tying thread, whip-finish and cement

Chapter 5

Creative Yarn-Body Dressings

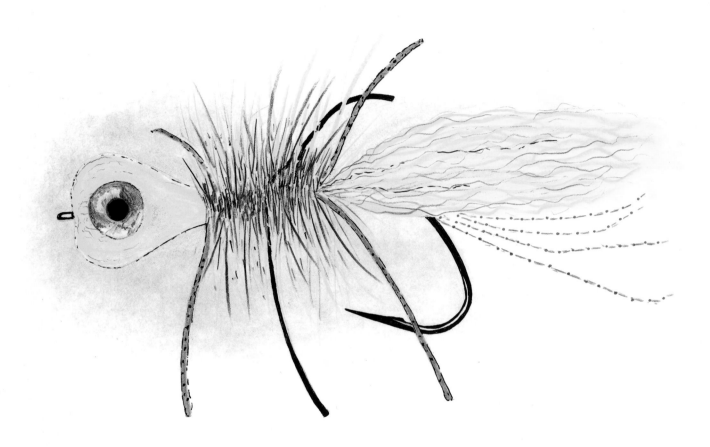

CREATIVE YARN-BODY DRESSINGS means exactly that. Not your typical fly-tying methods but perhaps a combination of techniques or simply a new spin-off method on an old standby pattern. What else can be done with poly yarn? I like to think I haven't exhausted all that can be done with it. The applications are many and now that polypropylene yarn is expanding into other fly-tying products we should be witnessing a new generation of fish-catching flies!

Clark's Stillborn Dun

The Stillborn Dun is yet another pattern designed to fulfill a fly-fishing objective. The challenge was to create a fly that would represent a big yellow mayfly working its way out of the nymphal shuck. After spending numerous minutes watching mayflies hatch, I observed a few noteworthy characteristics. I could see a tail, and the gills were quite visible. I could see part of a wing, and the body color was brownish. The next day I laid out all the tying materials I had with me on a picnic table and went to work selecting materials to match a hatching mayfly. I created a rendition of what I saw the night before, duplicating as close as pos-

sible the floating nymph I had observed.

That evening arrived and loaded with great expectation I rowed my boat out to one of my regular fishing spots. It was roughly four hours before the flies would begin emerging, but I just had to see what the new stillborn looked like on the water. The fly wasn't on the surface longer than three seconds when a twelve-inch rainbow exploded on it. Hatch or not, it has provided great fishing for me. Some of my fishing comrades have used it for other imitations, such as retrieving with a sinking line to suggest a leech or dragonfly nymph.

Clark's Stillborn Dun

Hook: Standard 3X long nymph hook, size 10

Thread: Tan, 6/0

Tail: Light brown poly yarn or brown and tan yarn mixed

Body: Same as tail

Gills: Buggy Nymph dubbing, #23 golden stone

Shellback: Same as tail

Wing post: Same as tail

Hackle: Brown saddle

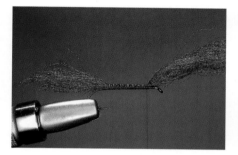

Step 1: Tie in the thread at front and cover the hook shank to the bend of the hook. Tie in a 6-inch length of single-strand yarn at the bend extending backward about 1 hook shank length. Return the thread to the front about 2 eye lengths back. Wrap the yarn forward and secure it tightly.

Step 2: Wrap the thread backwards over the yarn body in 7-9 loose wraps to the tail. Pull the yarn back over the body and secure tightly with thread wraps.

Step 3: In tying the gills, keep a loose wad of dubbing material in your non-tying hand with a sparse amount at the tips of your thumb and index fingers. Position the fibers alongside the yarn body and wrap over the ends of the fibers several times. Pluck the dubbing away from the body. The effect should be a tattered finished look as illustrated.

Step 4: Repeat on both sides of the body until 2/3 of the hook shank is covered. Note the taper of the gills from the tail to the front.

Step 5: Pull the yarn over the top of the body and gills as a shell back and secure firmly with the thread. Pull the yarn tight in a vertical posture and make tight thread wraps around the base to form the wing post.

Step 6: Wrap the hackle 3-4 times around the base of the post and tie off. Trim the wing post to within 1/4 inch of the hackle.

Step 7: Top view.

Step 8: Bottom view.

Brillo Bug

Chalk up another one for the bugger list! By using a dubbing loop and spinning the poly yarn, it is very simple to wrap it in between the glass beads. The shine of the poly yarn complements the sheen of the beads, producing a great visual for the predator. The yarn fibers give some counter-buoyancy to the beads so the fly won't drop like a rock, and the yarn is pliable enough to pulsate when stripped through the kill zone. The olive color is one of the best-fished patterns on many trout lakes!

Brillo Bug

Originator and tier: Joe Warren

Hook: 3X or 4X long streamer hook, sizes 6-10

Thread: Olive, 6/0

Body: 3-5 Killer Caddis caddis green glass beads, size large

Tail: Olive Bow Tyer, arctic fox tail

Dubbing: Olive poly yarn

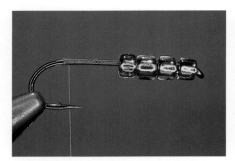

Step 1: Thread 4 glass beads onto the hook. Push the beads to the front of the hook and tie in the thread behind the beads. Wrap the thread over the hook shank to the bend.

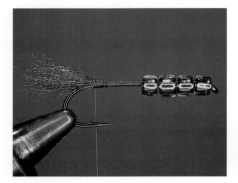

Step 2: Tie in a small foundation of yarn as a tail, about 1/3 the length of the hook shank.

Step 3: Tie in the arctic fox tail, one full hook length.

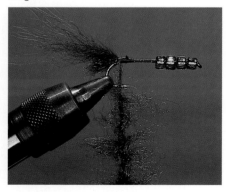

Step 4: At the front of tail, make a dubbing loop about 3 inches long. Cut the yarn into 3/4-inch pieces and use it for spinning in the dubbing loop (you can also blend the yarn as shown in Technique #2, page 9).

Step 5: Make several wraps with the dubbing loop ahead of the tail. Turn the hook upside down. Push one bead back to the dubbing wraps. Wrap the dubbing loop underneath the bead and around the hook making sure that the dubbing loop does not slip off to the side. Wrap the dubbing loop twice and push the next bead back to the dubbing wraps. Repeat the wrapping process until you have brought the dubbing loop to the front of the beads.

Step 6: Turn the hook upright, wrap the dubbing loop several more times at the front and tie it off. Complete the head with thread wraps and whip-finish.

Clark's Soft Body (S.B.) Plopper

The Soft Body Plopper originated like everything else I usually tie, playing around on the vise until something constructive appears. With a hook poised in the vise, like a blank canvas on an easel, I attached a small bundle of poly yarn allowing the filaments to revolve around the shank. I then added seven or eight tight wraps of thread to secure the bundle. For no reason at all, I began working the yarn to change its shape. With a pushing action, an elongated bubble appeared. A few hours of experimentation eventually lead to the pattern you see here. Soon after I discovered this technique I was introduced to Soft Body, a water-soluble plastic resin. The combination of poly yarn and Soft Body resulted in an obscure bubble with good floatation. This is the premise for the foundation of the fly, the rest is whatever you would like it to be. See Technique #8, page 14.

Clark's Soft Body (S.B.) Plopper

Hook: Stinger bass hook, size 2
Thread: Yellow, 3/0
Tail: Rainbow Krystal Flash and yellow poly yarn
Head: Yellow poly yarn
Legs: Rubber Hackle
Hackle: Chartreuse or yellow dyed grizzly
Eye: Yellow prismatic tape eyes
Head coating: Soft Body plastic resin, thin and thick recipes

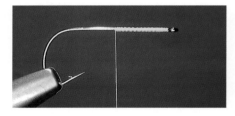

Step 1: Wrap the forward half of the hook with thread and leave thread at mid-point.

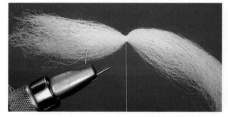

Step 2: Use 4-5 strands of poly yarn and place completely over and around the hook shank. Use a loose wrap of the thread to carefully roll the yarn around the hook to make sure that the yarn is completely surrounding the hook. Finish binding the yarn with tight thread wraps. Leave enough yarn material out the back of the hook to make the tail.

Step 3: Cover the yarn with the thread from the eye of the hook to the point. Leave the thread about midway on the body.

Step 4: Tease the yarn with your fingers to fashion the yarn 360° around the hook.

Step 5: Pull all of the yarn fibers to the back of the hook.

Step 6: To shape the head, experiment with the amount of tension when pulling the yarn. The harder you pull, the smaller the diameter of the head. Pushing the fibers toward the eye will produce more of a bubble. Once you create the shape of the head, bind the yarn with tight wraps of the thread.

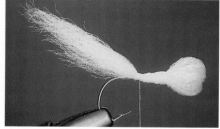

Step 7: Trim the yarn tail. Continue to wrap the thread tightly over the yarn to the back.

Step 8: Tie in the Krystal Flash along the thread base of the yarn tail. Tie in the legs between the tail and head, leave enough space to wrap in the hackle in between them.

Step 9: Apply a coat of the "thin" Soft Body over the yarn head. Let the resin dry completely for at least a few hours.

Step 10: Add the prismatic tape eyes. Apply a second coat of the "thick" Soft Body over the eyes and head and allow to dry.

Step 11: Tie in the hackle ahead of the tail and bring the thread to the front. Wrap the hackle forward and tie it off to complete the fly.

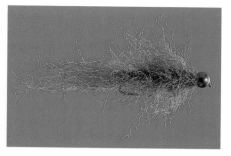

Bead Head Woolly Bugger, Rust
Tier: Gerry Clark
Hook: Standard wet 2X long, sizes 8 and 10
Thread: Orange 6/0
Tail: Rust, brown, and gold Clark's Tying Yarn mixed
Body: Rust, brown, and gold Clark's Tying Yarn dubbed
Head: Gold Bead

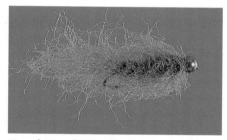

Bead Head Woolly Bugger, Olive
Tier: Gerry Clark
Hook: Standard wet 2X long, sizes 8 and 10
Thread: Olive 6/0
Tail: Olive Clark's Tying Yarn
Body: Olive Clark's Tying Yarn dubbed
Head: Gold Bead

Bead Head Woolly Bugger, Black
Tier: Gerry Clark
Hook: Standard wet 2X long, sizes 8 and 10
Thread: Black 6/0
Tail: Black Clark's Tying Yarn
Body: Black Clark's Tying Yarn dubbed
Head: Gold Bead

Edge Brite Butt Matuka

Hook: 6X long, size 4-8

Thread: Black 6/0

Tail: 4 strands of Krystal Flash and olive poly yarn

Butt: Orange Edge Brite over silver tinsel

Body: Olive poly yarn dubbed, the top half is brushed or picked out with a pin

Rib: Fine gold wire

Head: Black thread

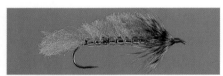

Glass Chub

Originator and tier: Joe Warren

Hook: Daiichi 2340, sizes 2-4

Thread: Olive 6/0

Body: 8 to 10 olive (silver-lined) beads, large

Tail: Olive Clark's Tying Yarn

Back: A small bundle of olive poly yarn is tied between each bead and tapered

Hackle: Olive

Bonefish Special, brown and white

Tier: Tim Borski

Hook: Standard saltwater, size 1

Thread: Monofilament 6/0

Butt: Pearl Crystal Chenille

Tail: Tan Fish Fur marked with brown pen

Body: Brown and white Clark's Tying Yarn placed alternately using the bundling technique on page 17

Eyes: Black, mono

Weed guard: 20-pound Mason hard monofilament

Bonefish Special, tan and white

Tier: Tim Borski

Hook: Standard saltwater, size 1

Thread: Monofilament 6/0

Tail: White Fish Fur marked with brown pen

Body: Tan and white Clark's Tying Yarn placed alternately using the bundling technique on page 17

Eyes: Bead chain

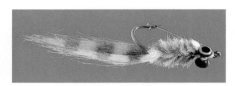

Bonefish Special, green and white

Tier: Tim Borski

Hook: Standard saltwater, size 1

Thread: Monofilament 6/0

Tail: Tan Fish Fur marked with brown strips then green on top

Body: Green and white Clark's Tying Yarn placed alternately using the bundling technique

Eyes: Lead dumbbell, painted

Weed guard: 20-pound Mason hard monofilament

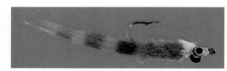

Bonefish Special, green, tan, and white

Tier: Tim Borski

Hook: Standard saltwater, size 1

Thread: Monofilament 6/0

Tail: Tan Fish Fur marked with brown strips

Body: Green and tan Clark's Tying Yarn placed alternately using the bundling technique on page 17, then a bundle of white on each side, at the front

Eyes: Lead dumbbell, painted

Weed guard: 20-pound Mason hard monofilament

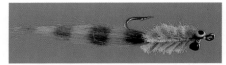

Bonefish Special, tan, white, and orange

Tier: Tim Borski

Hook: Standard saltwater, size 1

Thread: Monofilament 6/0

Tail: Tan Fish Fur marked with brown strips

Body: Tan and white Clark's Tying Yarn placed alternately using the bundling technique on page 17, then a bundle of orange on each side, at the front

Eyes: Lead dumbbell, painted

Weed guard: 20-pound Mason hard monofilament

Poly Scud

Hook: Wet fly, size 12-16

Thread: Orange 6/0

Body: Orange Clark's Tying Yarn dubbed, then picked out

Shellback: Orange Clark's Tying Yarn and Soft Body (Technique #3, page 10)

Rib: Gold wire

Note: The shellback is prepared and allowed to dry before attaching.

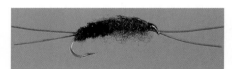

Clark's Poly Stone Nymph, black

Hook: Bent-shank nymph, 3X long, sizes 4-8

Thread: Black 6/0

Tail: Black rubber hackle

Body: The back half is large black Crystal Chenille, trimmed top and bottom, the forward half is black Clark's Tying Yarn dubbed and picked out

Wingcase: Three separate sections of black Clark's Tying Yarn coated with Soft Body and clipped to shape (Technique #3, page 10)

Head: Black thread

Antennae: Black rubber hackle

Note: The wingcase is prepared, allowed to dry, and cut to shape before attaching.

Clark's Poly Stone Nymph, brown

Hook: Bent-shank nymph, 3X long, sizes 4-8

Thread: Brown 6/0

Tail: Black rubber hackle

Body: The back half is large copper brown Crystal Chenille, trimmed top and bottom, the forward half is brown Clark's Tying Yarn dubbed and picked out

Wingcase: Three separate sections of brown Clark's Tying Yarn coated with Soft Body and clipped to shape (Technique #3, page 10)

Head: Brown thread

Antennae: Black rubber hackle

Note: The wingcase is prepared, allowed to dry, and cut to shape before attaching.

Clark's Poly Wing Stone

Hook: 2X long, sizes 6 and 8

Thread: Orange 6/0

Body: Gold tinsel

Underwing: Orange polypropylene yarn

Wing: Black and tan poly yarn is mixed, then Soft Body is applied and formed into a 3/8-inch wide strip. When dry, the strip is cut to shape (Technique #3, page 10)

Hackle: 1 brown saddle hackle

Clark's Pirate

Hook: Wide gap, 3X long, size 4

Thread: Black 6/0

Head: Purple or red Clark's Tying Yarn using the Yarn Shroud (Technique #8, page 14) and Soft Body

Tail: Purple Clark's Tying Yarn

Body: Red chenille

Hackle: Purple, palmered on the front half of the body, then wrapped as close as possible to the back of the head. Use 5 or 6 wraps of thread to down the hackle, then whip-finish behind the head

Eyes: Doll

Clark's Orange Soft Body Plopper

Hook: Wide gap, 3X long, size 4

Thread: Black 6/0

Head: Orange Clark's Tying Yarn using the Yarn Shroud (Technique #8, page 14) and Soft Body

Body: Orange Clark's Tying Yarn

Legs: Hot orange, Metallic Glitter Leggs

Collar: Black tying thread

Note: The body is the yarn left over after the head is formed.

Veiled Streamer, natural bait

Originators: Lee Clark and Joe Warren

Tier: Joe Warren

Hook: Daiichi Saltwater X-point, sizes 2-2/0

Thread: Gudebrod "G" white to start body, 3/0 black to finish

Body: Saltwater pearl Flashabou wrapped over white thread

Hackle tips: 3-4 grizzly saddle hackle, tied 1/3 of shank length behind eye

Veil: White poly yarn or Poly Bear

Wing: Gray and black poly yarn combed together or baitfish color Poly Bear

Cheeks: Gray poly yarn

Throat: Red poly yarn

Eyes: Prizma Tape Eyes, silver, 9/32

Note: Use Soft Body to finish over eyes and head, 1 coat of "thin," 2 coats of "thick."

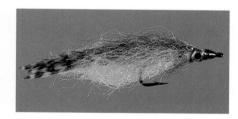

Veiled Streamer, chartreuse

Originators: Lee Clark and Joe Warren

Tier: Joe Warren

Hook: Daiichi 2451, sizes 2-2/0

Thread: Gudebrod 3/0, fluorescent chartreuse for body, black to finish

Body: Pearl saltwater Flashabou wrapped over chartreuse thread

Hackle tips: Olive or yellow dyed grizzly saddle, 3-4 each side

Veil: Chartreuse Clark's Tying Yarn combed thin

Wing: Baitfish color Poly Bear

Throat: Red Clark's Tying Yarn

Eyes: Prizma Tape Eyes, yellow, 7/32

Note: Use Soft Body plastic resin to coat head and eyes.

Chapter 6
The Adventures of the Clark's Stonefly

Deschutes River
"Railroad" Fly

MY STORY BEGINS IN JUNE 1976. Gene Strehlou, biology teacher at St. Helens High School, was in need of another adult to supervise a group of his students for a three-day float down the Deschutes River. It was my first time fly fishing the Deschutes and experiencing rowing down any whitewater river. It was also on this trip that I was introduced to the famous Deschutes stonefly hatch. I had no idea that this particular adventure would impact my life as much as it has.

The following year I decided that rowing down a river the size of the Deschutes was not for me. I enjoyed the fishing, camping, and the beauty of the river more, so my son Gerry and I teamed up with another father and son, Gene and Jim Frost, and hiked ten miles downriver from South Junction Train Station to White Horse Rapids. This one-week adventure was a time of togetherness with my son and a chance to study the characteristics and mannerisms of the stonefly.

Before this trip I spent a lot of time speaking with other fishermen and looking through fly-tying books and magazines searching for the best dry-fly pattern for this particular hatch. I decided on an orange Bucktail Caddis, and armed with two dozen we fished with only fair success. My caddis pattern, or at least the way I tied it, had two major flaws. Because of a sparse hackle and a high wing angle, the fly landed on its side most of the time. It was frustrating to make a decent cast and see a large Deschutes redside charge my offering, only to watch it come to a sudden halt, turn and disappear into the depths. It was this experience that motivated me to create a stonefly pattern.

In the eight years following, Gerry and I continued our one-week treks into the Deschutes canyon. With us on one of our trips was Butch Patterson, my brother-in-law and his two sons, Brian and Teddy. One only needs to mention the word Deschutes around Butch and he will recall any number of his fishing experiences. Gerry Tinkle, English teacher and track coach at St. Helens High School, also joined us for a couple of days during another trip. Without his expertise in English and supportive encouragement, I would not have attempted to write this book.

Those were memorable years for my son and me. Each excursion was filled with camping and fishing adventures but most importantly, it was a time of just sharing our lives with each other. An experience we shared was speaking with fishermen we encountered along the way. We learned a lot about the river from them. I enjoyed collecting adult stonefly patterns from our visitors. In all, I gathered eleven different imitations.

I acquired one of these from a railroad maintenance man we met on the tracks one day. The fly was tied with a single strand of synthetic yarn, knotted in the middle, doubled and tied on top of a bare hook. The drawing on the previous page shows the location of the knot. An elk-hair wing was added, followed by a brown saddle hackle. The fly was finished off with an orange head. For fear of losing this unique pattern, I did not fish it, but put it in a safe place with the notion that the fly would catch fish.

The summer of 1982 was the turning point for the development of my stonefly. While fishing Oregon's Metolius River, I observed a fisherman using a very interesting pattern. The simplicity of its design and appearance on the water's surface was very different from the other patterns I had collected. I asked if he had tied the pattern. He said no, an old man that he had met on the river gave it to him. With the image of the pattern etched in my mind, I wished the man good fishing and raced back to my camper to tie a couple flies for the afternoon fishing. The hook's shaft was wrapped with gold tinsel. Yellow dyed deer hair was tied on top of the hook followed by natural elk hair representing the wing as illustrated below. The gold tinsel and the impressionistic body represented by the yellow dyed deer-hair underwing attracted me, perhaps the trout would feel the same way.

After several minutes at the vise and a quick lunch, I was off again to try my newly discovered pattern. It worked well that day, producing a few nice fish. I was most impressed with its life-like appearance as it floated naturally downstream and that fish took the fly with abandon. If this pattern had a negative at all, it was the fact that it did not have a hackle, making it difficult to see on the water.

The following winter, while working with some of my art students on macramé—the art of knot tying—I noticed the poly cord we were using was fairly coarse in texture, more so than the poly yarn one sees in a fly-fishing shop. It was curiosity that led me to substitute the macramé yarn material for the deer-hair underwing of the previously described pattern. Separating the cord down into smaller strands and combing it was all the preparation needed.

The next summer, the first completed Clark's Stonefly touched the waters of the Deschutes and Metolius rivers. With immediate success, there was no doubt that I had accomplished what I set out to do.

Fishing the flats below White Horse Rapids on the Deschutes, I positioned myself downstream from a small ripple guarded by an island on one side and a large grass tuft on the other. With a size 6 rust-bodied Clark's Stonefly, I made two false casts and placed the fly several feet upstream into the ripple close to the grass hummock. Just as the fly approached the hummock, a large rainbow suddenly appeared under the fly, tracking it for a good two to three seconds before the take. The fish made one good run and two minutes later I released a hefty, eighteen-inch Deschutes redside. Over the past several years many fish have succumbed to the Clark's Stonefly but this particular fishing moment is the most unforgettable.

While fishing the Metolius I wanted to compare the proportions of the real insect with the pattern I had just finished, I took it from the vise and walked down to the river's edge. The Golden Stones were just beginning to appear in the grass and over hanging bushes. Cautiously, I approached an insect, snatched it quickly between my fingers and drew my pattern closer to compare. Without warning, the natural broke from

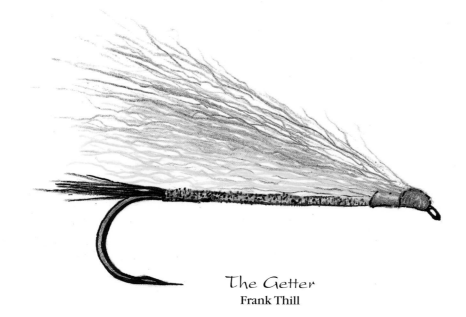

The Getter
Frank Thill

I heard the Clark's Stonefly was buggy...but can you believe this?

my grasp and jumped on top of the imitation. I couldn't believe what I was seeing. The insect was trying to mate with Clark's Stonefly.

The following winter I called Pete Rehnberg, a professional cartoonist who at the time was teaching school in Nehalem, Oregon. I asked him if he would create a cartoon that described this unusual phenomenon. He agreed, and gladly accepted two dozen Clark's Stoneflies for the payment.

Well, there you have it in a nutshell, the origin of the Clark's Stonefly. It was created first and foremost to fill a personal fishing need. Its development was accomplished by studying the characteristics and mannerisms of the insect, collecting adult stonefly patterns from fishermen, researching fly-fishing books and magazines, and lastly, tying and trying dozens of flies.

The summer of 1983 the Clark's Stonefly was in its completed form. It was such an effective pattern for me that I couldn't keep it to myself and began sharing it with everyone I met on the Deschutes and Metolius rivers. How's fishin'? What fly ya usin'? Have you tried

any stonefly patterns? These were typical questions I asked fishermen to begin a conversation and eventually lead to an introduction of my stonefly. Most people expressed some interest in my pattern, especially when I offered them a free one to try. No one refused! To check reactions to the fly's success, I always exchanged names and addresses with those that accepted my stonefly. Some early contacts have developed into lasting friendships. One of these special contacts is Mark Avolio, one of the first fishermen I introduced the Clark's Stonefly to on the Metolius. If I'm not mistaken, Mark was predominately a wet-fly fisherman until he saw his first fish rise to the Clark's Stonefly. He has been using my pattern for many years in different fishing situations beyond the Deschutes and Metolius rivers. He writes:

"I want to take this opportunity to let you know how successful your various fly patterns have been for me. I have been using the Clark's Stonefly since I first met you on the Metolius River in

1981. Since then, I have fished the Clark's Stonefly in Oregon, Idaho, Montana, Alberta and Washington State. In all cases, the Clark's Stonefly has produced consistent, almost unbelievable success. In one instance, where I knew fish were holding, I tried using a foam body stonefly pattern and then tried a woven body stonefly pattern with no success. I then tried a Clark's Stonefly and caught fish on the next four casts. I have said it before and I will say it again: I honestly believe trout will take the Clark's Stonefly over a natural. I have also found it to be an excellent October Caddis imitation. In fact, it has worked as a grasshopper imitation on the second meadow of Slough Creek and as a Damsel Fly on Grebe Lake.

I have also had the opportunity to try your caddis fly patterns and they work as good as the stonefly pattern. I have tried the Clark's Caddis on the Deschutes, Rogue, Madison,

Yellowstone and Slough Creek. The Clark's Caddis, just like the Clark's Stonefly is a true inter mountain West pattern.

Another great pattern is the Clark's Stonefly tied on a size 14 or 16 hook. This variation is an excellent imitation of the Little Yellow Sally. The pattern has been particularly effective on the Deschutes and Madison Rivers and Grebe Lake for both trout and grayling."

I continued my one-man crusade by showing my pattern to many fly-fishing shop clerks and managers. During one such visit, in Salem, Oregon, the clerk liked the appearance of the fly so much that he wanted to show it to another employee who wasn't there at the time. I gladly gave him a couple flies but had some doubts where this contact would lead. A few days later I received a letter from John Shewey, the absent employee:

Dear Mr. Clark,
"Thank you for stopping in at Fishing Outfitters on November 10 to show us your stonefly imitation. I like your innovative idea and am perfectly willing to push the popularity of your fly among my constituents. I can't wait to try it out myself on next year's hatch.

I am a writer and have written an outdoor column for a local paper for several years. Several times I have devoted my space to flyfishing with good response from many readers. Therefore, I would like to write something about your fly but I will need some complete information to do so. If possible I would like a complete history of your fly as well as some of your insights into the use of the Clark's Stone. This may require a little time on your part, but if my publishers like the idea, the exposure will be beneficial since the circulation of the paper for which I write, covers

the Santiam River Canyon, a major gateway to the Deschutes country."

Very excited about the opportunity of having my pattern published, I sent John a cassette tape filled with historical information and tying instructions. Several weeks later I received a short letter saying that he decided not to submit the article to his local newspaper but to present it to *Flyfishing* magazine. He further reported that it was accepted by the publisher and would appear in print within two years.

For me those two years seemed like an eternity, but the day finally arrived. Exactly two years after the initial contact with John, the 1986 June issue bearing the Clark's Stonefly appeared on the newsstand. Because this issue is no longer in print, and difficult to find, I have included most of it here.

Fly Wrap Up, Clark's Stonefly

Fly shop employees are introduced to a smorgasbord of different "killer patterns," and being, or at least acting optimistic, about every new bug carried in the door is all part of a day's work. So, when Lee Clark asked me to take a look at his stonefly imitation, I readied my, "yeah, I bet that fly really knock's em dead," routine.

Lee's bug was something different, though, and I honestly took an interest in the fly. I could picture the way it would ride the water and the way trout would respond. Lee left me a fistful of Clark's Stones and a business card sporting the tag "Windy Acres Fly Shop."

When my June date with the lower Deschutes River arrived, I had two dozen Clark's Stones dressed and ready to go. The first day of the float trip found me hesitant to use the new pattern. I stuck with my old favorite, the Jughead, and caught

fish. The big *Pteronarcys* and *Acroneuria* stones never developed into a big production as persistent clouds dumped occasional rain flurries and a gusting wind kept the temperature down.

Up early the second morning, I went brush-busting along the river bank. I pinpointed a persistent feeder holding below overhanging branches. I squeezed a short bow cast through the trees and watched my Jughead float over the fish unmolested. On the second cast, I lightly jigged the fly on the surface as it cut downstream. The rainbow's silvery sides flashed inches below the surface, indicating a sudden change of mind just before slamming the fly.

I tried the same thing again and nothing happened. I gave the fish a rest. Five minutes later, I sacrificed a live golden stone to relocate the trout. The struggling natural disappeared in a sudden swirl. I counted off 60 seconds and dropped my Jughead onto the water. Again I saw the metallic flash of a turning fish.

A bit frustrated by now, I decided it was time to give Lee's bug a serious workout. I selected one of the golden stone imitations. One short bow cast and five minutes later, I released a fat 17-inch redside. I experimented for the next two days and the Clark's Stone outfished my Jugheads in a bad way. Those finicky devils that flat refused any other stonefly patterns usually got stung with Lee's bug.

Clark's Stone looks buggy. It rides flush on the water and penetrates the surface film well to closely represent the natural. The macramé yarn underwing soaks up a little water to enhance the fly's bugginess and the gold body adds a touch of flash.

Tying the Clark's Stone is simple—another nice feature of the pattern."

For several weeks following, I received letters from all over the United States requesting flies or the macramé yarn to tie them. The last letter I received came from Pat Trotter, a freelance writer. He requested some yarn and an opportunity to interview me for an article. One year after our interview, an article entitled "Clark's Stonefly, Caddis and Hopper," appeared in the July 1987 issue of *Salmon Trout Steelheader* magazine. Part of the article mentioned Gary Kish who, at the time of the article, worked at the Camp Sherman Store and Fly Shop on the Metolius River. Pat Trotter indicated that Gary mentioned the Clark's Stonefly several times in his weekly column in *The Nugget*, the local newspaper. He also singled out my pattern in his periodic reports to *Fishing and Hunting News*. Most noteworthy was Gary's personal testimony regarding my pattern, he writes:

"The Clark Stone is one of the most effective patterns for imitating hatches of golden stoneflies and salmonflies. Its combined traits of durability, floatability, effectiveness and ease of tying are unmatched by other patterns I've used. The effectiveness is in large part due to the fly perfectly duplicating the natural's surface attitude and silhouette.

This past summer while fishing the legendary Deschutes salmonfly hatch, I watched in amazement as large redsides ignored naturals that I tossed to them to eagerly take Clark's Stones that I presented with downstream casts.

On my home river, the Metolius, the local "Salmonfly" hatch of golden stones lasts a full three months. During this time a Clark's Stone fished tight to the bank, drag-free, and given an occasional twitch, never fails to produce trout and often very good trout at that—sixteen to twenty inches, that feed very selectively.

Good floatability on the Metolius' swift broken water means more fish caught each day because less time is spent dressing and drying sodden flies; another reason the Clark Stone is a favorite of mine. I spend more time fishin' and less time fussin'."

Four months later in the same magazine, Mr. Trotter, in an article entitled "Fall Caddis Time," featured the Clark's Stonefly with five other dry imitations for the adult caddis.

Sometime in the fall of 1988, Brad Weigandt, one of my art students, brought several copies of *Western Outdoors* magazine to show me the fly-tying section. He suggested that I should submit the Clark's Stonefly to Mr. John McKim, the writer of the "Fly Ideas" column. Within two days I sent a letter of introduction and a fly sample to the magazine and one week later received a reply from Mr. McKim:

"As to your fly. Strange how things have a way of working out. Only recently I was looking for a fly to feature when I ran across one sent to me by Craig Lacy in Bend. Not as a prospective pattern, but as an example of what I should tie for a two-day float my son and I were taking down the Deschutes with Craig last May. You guessed it. It was the "Clark's Stonefly," although Craig did not name the fly or give any details. Just said it was a fantastic pattern for that river.

Now that I know its originator and other details, I'm delighted at the opportunity to use it in my column, perhaps as soon as the April 89 issue. As a matter of fact I am always looking for good—preferably unique—patterns."

The 1989 March issue of *Western Outdoors* appeared on the newsstand containing an article about the Clark's Stonefly. The exciting thing about this contact is, Mr. McKim has invited me to submit other fly patterns for his column.

Having been a subscriber to *Flyfishing* magazine for many years, it was a habit of mine to turn first to the "Angler's Catch and Release Gallery" section where photos of fishermen releasing a fish were shown. In the 1989 April issue what I had hoped for happened. The picture shows Dr. Ed Rizzolo of Pearland, Texas holding a hefty trout he caught and released on the Green River in Utah. Tackle used to make the catch was a Fisher GT-40, 9-foot rod, 4-5 weight line, Pfleuger Medalist reel, and, you guessed it, Clark's Golden Stonefly pattern. Shortly after I saw the picture, I called Marty Sherman, the magazine's editor at the time, and requested Dr. Rizzolo's mailing address, without hesitation Marty gave it to me. I sent the doctor a letter of introduction and a Clark's Stonefly to begin a dialogue that continues today. He writes:

"I read the article about your pattern in the June 1986 issue of *Flyfishing*. I rather liked its simplicity and so I tied a few. Everyone I showed them to seemed to like them, so I tied them in different sizes from #12 to #6, some with orange macramé, and some with light yellow that I darkened with a Pantone pen to a golden yellow color. I use dark or light deer hair for the wings. I usually tie it exactly as you do except on my patterns I tried to put a little more macramé and a little less deer hair, (only because I had not seen yours before). On a few of them, I have only added one minor modification (which is really not necessary), I tie a small

sizes I'm sure it can resemble a caddis.

I also use it in Texas for bass and panfish (bluegill, sunfish etc.). It works just fine fishing around the edges of small ponds."

Besides a medical practice, Dr. Rizzolo is active as a fly-tying instructor in Texas Flyfishers of Houston. I know that when the doctor has an opportunity, he shares the Clark's Stonefly with his classes and the Federation of Fly Fishers conclaves. Because of his popularity and influence, one of his sessions was published in the June 1989 Texas Flyfishers' newsletter. Included here is just the first part of the article:

"At the last meeting, Ed Rizzolo was good enough to tie Clark's Stone Fly for us. According to the good doctor, this is a real fish getter. This is not the usual line of malarkey accompanying a newly discovered fly, for he has pictures, proof positive, taken by a reasonably honest photographer, Ken Jacoby.

The fly was created by Lee Clark, a high school art teacher and owner of the Windy Acres Fly Shop in St. Helens, Oregon. It took Lee 10 years to develop the fly as it exists today. He first fished it on the famed Deschutes River. Later it proved its worth on the Metolius River in the Camp Sherman, Oregon, area. Lee says that while it is primarily a stonefly imitation, it also works well as a caddis pattern.

Lee's list of materials is short and his tying instructions are quite simple. Anyone of our students who completed the beginners class this spring would find it an easy pattern to tie."

tuft of moose hair on the back end of the fly.

I was fishing the middle stretch of the Green River and had floated to a point where a creek had entered and made the river somewhat murky. The guide, Terry Collier, who has the "Ole Moe" guide service had me fishing a large hopper fly and I caught several nice fish on it. Things slowed down a little and that's when I decided to try your stonefly. I read that there is a hatch of Golden Stoneflies on the Green River but I think it had

already taken place. The guide didn't think much of the fly. On my first cast about 6 inches from the bank, I caught that nice brown trout seen in the picture. On the next two casts I caught two more nice fish, where upon the guide wanted to take another look at my fly and wanted to know how it was tied. I caught many fish on your fly that day and the following two days.

I believe some fish take it for a hopper when fished close to the bank as they take it quickly after it hits the water. In smaller

One year later, the same article appeared in "Long Casts," the newsletter of the Southern Council Federation of

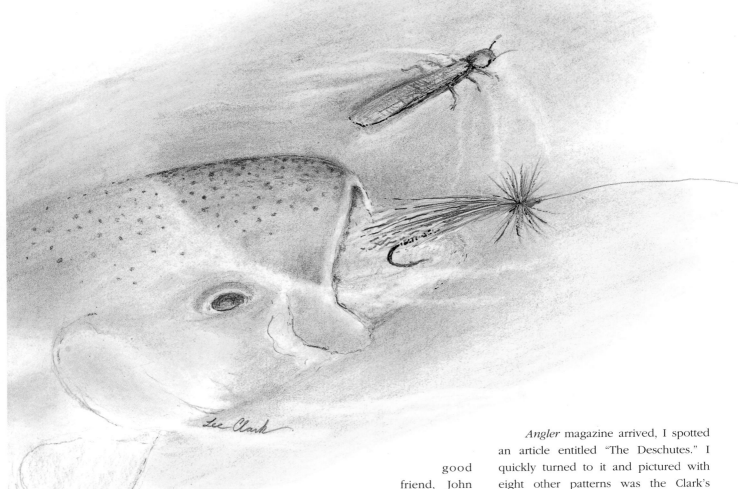

Fly Fishers. Soon after the publication of the article Ed sent me a short letter in which he stated:

"I just got a copy of the Federation's *Southern Council bulletin*. They have a whole page spread on Norm Crook's "Fit To Be Tied" article on the *Clark's Stonefly*. Man are you getting popular——that happens to go to clubs in 12 states."

Dr. Rizzolo is truly an ambassador for the Clark's Stonefly.

In the 1989 Fall issue of *American Angler & Fly Tier*, yet another article appeared. This time Clark's Stone was featured with eleven other flies in an article entitled "Topside Steelhead" by my good friend, John Shewey. His article presented very clearly the differences between skating flies and waking flies. With all the publicity thus far I wondered if it was possible to have my pattern published in *Fly Fisherman* magazine. I sent a half dozen Clark's Stoneflies and an introductory letter to Mr. John Randolph, the Editor and Publisher. Sometime in March, I received a nice thank you letter from Mr. Randolph. He expressed a great deal of interest in the pattern as a possible feature in his magazine. Since I had never written a magazine article and did not know the proper format required for submission, I contacted John Shewey and he graciously agreed to write the piece. In the 1991 December issue, the article appeared. The Clark's Stonefly was listed on the cover and featured in the fly-tying section in full color.

Surprises continued! When the 1992 January/February issue of *American Angler* magazine arrived, I spotted an article entitled "The Deschutes." I quickly turned to it and pictured with eight other patterns was the Clark's Stonefly. I noticed under the photograph of flies that Bill Krpalek from Eugene, Oregon tied them. It had been my pleasure to meet Bill a couple of years before at the Northwest Fly Tyers Exposition in Eugene. Since his phone number appeared in the article, I gave him a ring to express a word of thanks. Bill said that Scott Ripley, the writer of the Deschutes article, asked him to submit some flies used on the Deschutes. Because of his confidence in the pattern, Bill included the Clark's Stonefly. Good people like Bill Krpalek have contributed greatly to the popularity of my pattern.

To my surprise when the July 1992 issue of *Fly Fisherman* magazine arrived in the mail, the Clark's Stonefly was published again. This time it appeared in a piece entitled "Surface Flies For Steelhead" by Deke Meyer. The article featured fly patterns that deliver varying amounts of wake because of differences in fly design. There was one mistake in the article. The underwing material as listed in the recipe for my pattern was Sparkle Yarn, but of course, polypropylene macramé cord is used.

The St. Helens Safeway store is an enjoyable place to visit. One day as I accompanied my wife, Betty, I informed her I was going to pay a visit to the magazine department. The 1993 April/May issue of *Salmon Trout Steelheader* caught my eye. I opened to Pat Trotters article entitled, "Springtime Dries for the Deschutes". You guessed it! Clark's Stonefly was featured with a picture and some very nice words. In his article, Pat writes:

"The most-used salmonfly imitation in my book is the Clark Stonefly, a creation of Lee Clark of St. Helens, Oregon. This is the fly that goes on my leader when the fish are lurking in the pockets close to shore, waiting to pick off any hapless stonefly that might drop off the overhanging foliage. This is also the fly I use as my standard of comparison for testing new patterns. If I get more positive takes—or as positive for that matter—on the new pattern relative to the Clark'Stonefly, then I deem the new pattern a very good one indeed. But that seldom happens, which is why the Clark Stonefly has become my workhorse."

I have probably missed an article or two featuring my pattern, but to my knowledge, the last appeared in the 1997 Summer issue of *Fly Tying* magazine. The article entitled "The Wonders of Macramé Yarn: The Clark's Stonefly and Friends" by Joe J. Warren, was not a surprise. I gave Joe some background information, tied a few flies, and he put it all together in an excellent article.

Since 1986, Clark's Stonefly appeared in almost every fly-fishing magazine in the county and was featured in many Federation of Fly Fishers club newsletters and newspapers. The first book appearance occurred in *Meeting and Fishing the Hatches* by Charles Meck, published by Stephen Greene Press/ Pelham Books in 1991. Clark's Stonefly was not pictured but was described in detail. My pattern was credited for being effective on the Rogue River in Oregon.

The second, *Advanced Flyfishing For Steelhead* by Deke Meyer was published in May of 1992. Clark's Stone was presented in full color with other dry steelhead flies and there was a picture of me tying flies. In December of 1992, Randy Stetzer's book, *Flies: The Best 1,000* was published. The book featured the Clark's Stonefly plus five other patterns: Clark's Little Yellow Stone, Clark's Deer Hair Caddis, Clark's Hopper, Clark's Green Drake Parachute, and Clark's Big Yellow Mayfly.

Since *Flies: The Best 1000* others have been published, including the following titles:
Hatch Guide for the Lower Deschutes River, By Jim Schollmeyer.
Hatch Guide for Lakes, by Jim Schollmeyer.
Hatch Guide for Western Streams, by Jim Schollmeyer.
The Art of Tying the Dry Fly, by Skip Morris.
Flies for Trout, by Dick Stewart and Farrow Allen.
Fish Flies: Volume One by Terry Hellekson.
Dry Fly Fishing, by Dave Hughes.
Mastering the Spring Creeks, by John Shewey.
Western Streamside Guide, by Dave Hughes.
Trout Flies, by Dave Hughes.

In the process of all the magazine articles and books being published, the computer was rapidly making its way into the homes of America. Would Clark's Stonefly some day appear on the Internet? Would it sometime in the future be featured on CD ROM? About 1994, my son Gerry, while surfing the web, informed me that he did indeed locate it on a couple web pages. In 1995, "Great Rivers of the West"—developed by Virtual AdVentures, Seattle, Washington— one of the first CD ROM programs on fly fishing, hit the market. Clark's Stonefly was presented with other flies for the Deschutes River. In 1998, "Fishing Flies of North America" by Dick Stewart and Farrow Allen was produced. It included the entire five book series: *Flies for Trout, Atlantic Salmon, Saltwater, Bass and Panfish,* and *Steelhead.*

In addition to all the magazine articles, books, CD ROM programs, and the World Wide Web, personal appearances influenced the popularity of the Clark's Stonefly. One of the most enjoyable but stressful experiences was tying flies at the sportsman's shows in Portland, Oregon. Because my pattern was well known on the Metolius, the Camp Sherman Store and Fly Shop invited me to tie flies in their booth in 1987 and 1988. This was my first experience of demonstrating fly tying in public, and boy was it scary. I might add, I don't remember ever cutting my tying thread accidentally so I must not have been too nervous. In 1989, Keith Burkhart, President of the Oregon Council of Federation of Fly Fishers invited me to tie flies in their booth. One show attendee, LeRoy Hyatt, a writer for the *Lewiston Tribune*, of Lewiston, Idaho reported his visit to the show:

"After watching an impressive casting demonstration by Doug Swisher, my oldest son, Kevin, and I found a concession stand and bought a cold drink and large bag of popcorn.

After finishing our popcorn and drinks, we again started walking and looking. We stopped to watch a young man tying flies in a booth for the local chapter of the Fly Fishing Federation. Lee Clark of St. Helens, Ore., was explaining a fly of his own design. The enthusiasm with which he spoke of the Clark's Stonefly caught my attention.

In experimenting with his new creation, he told me of trout

that would take the Clark's Stonefly when other patterns failed.

One large trout followed the large stonefly for several feet before taking the fly with a slashing strike. That fish and several others fell for this new pattern on the Deschutes River that day.

The Clark's Stonefly also has been used successfully on many other streams and rivers in Oregon and Washington. The pattern now is being tested on some streams back east.

The independent body does seem to give a very good action in the water. Because the body only is secured at the front of the fly, the body is somewhat free to move with the current, giving the fly a different look."

I was amused that LeRoy described me as a young man. The truth is, at the time of this show I was fifty years old. The sportsman's shows not only gave me opportunities to introduce hundreds of fishermen to the Clark's Stonefly, but also opened doors of opportunity for me. Most likely because of my gift of gab, Mr. Burkhart offered me an invitation to the first-ever Northwest Fly Tyers Exposition in Eugene, Oregon, in March of 1989. It was an honor for me to be included with 39 of the best fly tiers in this part of the country. Several weeks after the Eugene event I received a phone call from Dan Byford, world-renowned for his Zonker pattern, and the Fly Tying Theater Director for the International Sportsmen's Exposition. According to Dan, Keith Burkhart recommended me as a guest tier for the up-and-coming show. Without hesitation, I accepted his invitation. When showtime arrived, I learned very quickly that teaching in front of a video camera was totally different from the classroom I was used to. All instruction is centralized to a television screen. The speaker's voice is necessary, but if there isn't something constantly happening to the fly, some

viewers get up and move on. My wife, Betty, a keen observer, pointed this out after my first experience. At the time of this writing, I have had the opportunity to tie flies in the I.S.E. show for the last eleven years.

From the very beginning of the Clark's Stonefly adventure, I have met some wonderful people, and my story wouldn't be complete without sharing how I met some of them.

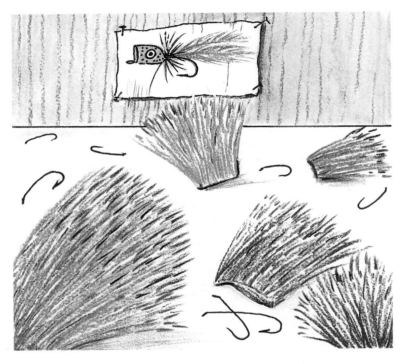

In the spring of 1986, St. Helens High School had the distinct pleasure of having Governor Victor Atiyeh as a guest speaker. I had read in a newspaper article that he was an avid fly fisherman and enjoyed fishing the Deschutes River. In the article the Governor admitted he was not a purist and would trim the bottom of his flies without a second thought. As he was leaving our school, I presented him with a box containing a half dozen Clark's Stoneflies. He graciously accepted my gift and promised to write me a letter. My final comment to him was that he did not need to trim the bottoms of the flies because I had already done it. It is a major characteristic of my pattern. July 6, 1987 I received this letter:

"I am much too tardy in telling you how successful the Clark's Stoneflies were in my not-too-often fishing ventures. For that I apologize, because they have worked very well. Since your letter of October last year I have had two fishing trips, both very recently at the end of June. Prior to that I had one occasion to use the flies you gave me, that in

early June. Because of the hatch they were the most productive in this latter outing, the early June trip finding the salmonfly versions most useful. You will be most interested to know that the trout were feeding just below the surface on rising flies from the bottom and were very choosy on anything presented to them. I tried many dry and wet flies and was most successful with yours.

Also of special interest to me was that the flies you tied hold together very well. As you know, sometimes we get flies that look good, but fade fast after a few casts, which is most discouraging."

The following winter I called Governor Atiyeh at his Portland residence to see if he needed any flies for the following season. He ordered a couple dozen Clark's Stoneflies and again promised to write. July 31, 1989 I received this letter:

"Just a note to tell you the flies I purchased prior to Christmas were finally laid on the water of the Deschutes. The orange bodied ones were sensational in the middle of June, but were replaced by a size 12 and 14 Elk Hair Caddis the early part of July.

During the earlier trek I got a lot of action and hooked my largest ever, 19 inches, during that trip."

I am truly thankful for the Governor's wonderful testimonies and special gift, a commemorative bronze coin bearing the State Seal on one side and his name inscribed on the other.

The day I met Mike Marchando will always be special to me. While fishing one of my special spots on the Metolius River in the summer of 1987, I noticed another fisherman working the water across and upstream from my location. As he approached, I hooked a feisty 10-inch rainbow and carefully released him. With curiosity, he asked what fly I was using. Of course I quickly replied, Clark's Stonefly. He stated that he read the article in *Flyfishing* magazine, tied a few but hadn't given them a try yet. I

strongly suggested that he give the pattern a go and further added that I was Clark. With a surprised look on his face, and no hesitation, the stranger crossed the river and promptly introduced himself as Mike Marchando. After several minutes of getting acquainted, Mike, being a part-time photographer, expressed an interest in snapping a few shots of my pattern with the natural insect. Because Mike was willing to use some of his film for the sake of the Clark's Stonefly, I gladly accepted his generosity and walked up stream to his campsite. Mike introduced me to his wife, Elsie, then grabbed his camera and we headed for the streamside vegetation. It was several weeks later when I received a package from Mike containing the photographs. They are some of my most treasured items of the Clark's Stonefly adventure.

I credit Mike Marchando for doing many things to promote the Clark's Stonefly and me as a fly tier. From the day we met on the river, Mike has introduced many people to the Clark's Stonefly. As a fly-tying instructor, Mike begins his students with tying of the Clark's Stonefly rather than the traditional Wooly Worm. He feels that it is relatively simple to tie, and with it they can experience fishing success with a fly pattern they have personally tied.

In 1990 Mike introduced me to Bob Borden, the owner of Hareline Dubbin, one of the largest wholesalers of fly-tying materials in the country. For approximately five years I supplied Hareline

Dubbin with my special yarn which was marketed to as far away as Japan.

About the same time, Mike gave a few Clark's Stoneflies to Kim Short, at the time, President of McKenzie Fly Tackle Company. After Kim discovered its effectiveness, he made contact with me and I became a contract tier with McKenzie from 1989 to 1997. Clark's Stoneflies were marketed throughout the United States.

As I stated earlier in my story, one of the fly patterns I was attracted to during the development stage was tied by a man who summered on the Metolius River. In the summer of 1987, just two days after I met Mike Marchando, I finally met the man. I had just finished a day of fishing downriver from Allingham Bridge on the Metolius. As was the custom, I stopped on the bridge to rest my weary feet and chit chat with other fishermen.

One of these, a very distinguished-looking gentleman sporting a white mustache and wearing a hat laden with many flies, was speaking with another fisherman. Approaching the two, I noticed the older man had what I thought was a Clark's Stonefly on his leader. Well, I opened my big mouth and asked him if he was using a Clark's Stonefly. To my amazement he answered no. It was a pattern he started tying 38 years ago. He later told me the name of his fly was "The Getter." A closer look at the fly verified that I had come face to face with the man that summered on the Metolius. His name was Frank Thill. I introduced myself and expressed my appreciation concerning his influence in the development of the Clark's Stonefly. Frank was very happy and flattered that I gave him a lot of credit for the pattern. I shall never forget him.

Bob Long, Jr. is another man I met during my "great adventure." How I met him is a story I know you will enjoy.

It was Christmas 1993, one of the our favorite seasons of the year, when we celebrate the birth of our Lord Jesus Christ and exchange gifts with our family and close friends. For Christmas my son gave me a Fly-fishing calendar. It featured twelve beautiful fishing scenes and a full page of photographed fishing flies. Of course I was struck by the fly photos and thought that perhaps someday Clark's Stonefly could be published in a calendar like this one. Since the photographers name and phone number were included with the photos, I gave him a call. After introducing myself to Mr. Bob Long, Jr. I asked if it was possible to submit my stonefly pattern for inclusion in the calendar. He stated that he was only contracted to take the pictures. Immediately I felt I hit a dead end! As it turned out, we became fly-tying pen pals.

Bob was an independent television producer/director for the City of Chicago and fishing-related photographer specializing in outdoor action, scenics, tabletop still-lifes, and advertising. Bob is also an artist, writer, and fly tier, but his main passion is fly fishing for smallmouth bass.

Since his writing is so entertaining and useful, I kept all his letters. Following are excerpts worth sharing from some of them. I was indeed flattered by what he had to say about me as a fly tier.

"AND THE WINNER IS....
Let me pass out the accolades while I should, while we're alive to hear them. You tie a sweet fly, my man. These flies of yours are a delight to look at. Nicely executed, neatly tied, well proportioned, but not fussily or overly designed."

I originally designed Clark's Stonefly to be a dry fly, and when I received his comments about how he fished it, I was shocked.

"Your fly works wonderfully for steelhead. They are tied on dry fly hooks, sizes 6 or 4, I don't remember off hand, and they have a very seductive bugginess under the water. The yarn supplies the color, the tinsel supplies the flash, and the hair supplies a puffy wingy look.

Remember I am drifting these with a noodle rod (10.5 - 12 ft. long) with 4 or 6 lb. test leader. As the weight bounces lightly along the bottom, the Stonefly just eases downstream and then swings across. Sometimes the fish hit it as it rises off the bottom as I begin to reel in. Now that is a strike! These steelies run from 7 - 12 lbs. and they put up quite a wonderful fight. Clark's Stonefly takes the licking and keeps on fishing. It has great durability and can last through 3 - 5 fish before it's either torn up or lost.

I usually try to modify all patterns that come before my bench, to make them more effective for our fishing. Except for size, Clark's Stonefly requires no modifications. It's a dandy pattern Lee."

In another letter, Bob made some comments about poly yarn:

"I admit I am somewhat slow to react to new materials sometimes. It may take me months looking at it, feeling it, thinking about it before the lightning bolt strikes and fly tying ideas begin to germinate.

This yarn of yours is a marvelous material that requires thoughtful consideration if one is to attempt to do justice to it. I gave away all of my first generation ties of Clark's Stonefly because I wanted to redo them. Then I gave away all of my Aunt Lydia's Rug Yarn, (which I had used as winging material). Although I don't design flies that float, they need a measure of buoyancy, (neutral or otherwise). Clark's Yarn has proven most effective. Its also got color translucency, body, shagginess and takes a colored marker well. (no running of color or wearing off in the water). It has been a useful and attractive addition to some of the patterns I fiddle around with."

The last story I will share is how I accidentally met a nationally known fly tier. On October 20, 1996, I was invited to tie flies at the Rainland Fly Casters club in Astoria, Oregon. I thought it would be a typical speaking engagement with me being the evening's program. Mid-way through my tying program I declared that I use inexpensive saddle hackles for my patterns. This statement caused the following dialogue:

Chuck Cameron: That's not a Hoffman number 1 premium then?

Me: No! This is one he wouldn't even show!

(Short pause.)

Me: Mine is probably rated a number 10.

Ron Reinebach: I just got something in the mail the other day that Henry made another award.

Me: Yeah, in the Oregon Council Newsletter! It was given to him back in Kalispell, Montana.

Ron Reinebach: Congratulations!

Henry Hoffman: Well, thank you.

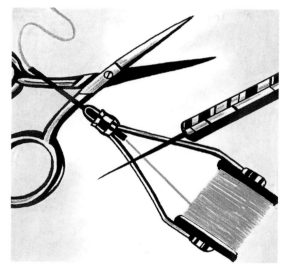

(I looked across the table to see who Ron was speaking to and suddenly realized that *the* Henry Hoffman was there.)

Me: Oh! It's you!

(I immediately reached across and began shaking Henry's hand. I quickly fanned myself and said), "Boy! Am I sweating now!"

(At this point, my program was out of control.)

Me again: I saw your picture and the article said you were from Warrenton, Oregon. I thought that was neat!

(Short pause)

Me: I had no idea that you would be here. That's fantastic!

(end of dialogue)

Very soon after my demonstration, Henry and I had the opportunity to get better acquainted and from that evening, we have stayed in contact. Anyone who has met Henry Hoffman will agree that he is a true gentleman with a great smile—and a man of few words.

Now, if you don't know who Henry Hoffman is, Joe Warren, in an article he wrote for the 1997 Fall issue of *Fly Tying* magazine, states:

"Henry, an avid fly Tier/fisherman, feather-man extraordinaire, and genetic engineer of the original Hoffman Super Grizzly, has spent nearly 30 years cultivating roosters for fly tying. He has the reputation of producing some of the finest dry-fly hackle in the world. Not only has he mastered dry-fly hackle but the production of wet-fly hackle as well. Henry claims his success in the hackle business is largely due to being a fly tier first and chicken farmer second.

The culmination of his career and devotion to fly fishing was celebrated with one of fly fishing's highest merits, The Lee Wulff Award, in 1994, by the Federation of Fly Fishers."

If you ever have the opportunity to meet Henry Hoffman, you will discover as I have that he is real gentleman. I am pleased to call him a friend.

To conclude the "adventure of Clark's Stonefly," I would like to share some good things Clark's Stonefly has done besides catch a lot of fish, and give fishing pleasure to thousands like yourself. The fly has been used to raise money for the Federation of Fly Fishers, the Oregon Council of the FFF, a conservation project in California, for Toy and Joy, Food Banks, and other worthy charities. You can honestly say that Clark's

Stonefly has done a lot of giving and taking from the beginning.

Throughout this "great adventure," you have been entertained with many interesting testimonies. I close now with one that is most precious. If you are a parent or grandparent you will appreciate this one very much. Eight-year-old Andrew Tainter, the son of John Tainter, drafting instructor at St. Helens High School, caught a fish one day using a Clark's Stonefly. I asked John if he could have his son write a short story about what happened. Two days later I received Andrew's well-written report:

"When I was six years old, I went to my second fishing derby. I was excited when I got there. My dad and I went to get a fishing pole and worms. After a while we found out, that didn't work, so my dad went to get the Clark's Stonefly. When I started to reel in, there was a big fish on my line. Would you believe it, I won first place in my division and won a big trophy.

Andrew Tainter
Eight years old."

Looking back, the hobby of fly tying was my way of unwinding after teaching high school students all day. It helped me as an only child to cope with the losses of my mother, father, and father-in-law. It was a way for me to explore the artistic side of my personality. As my friends will tell you, I am a non-traditional artisan who sees possibilities in every-day objects such as using the flash of a potato chip bag for tinsel. I am always experimenting and dreaming up new ways of applying non-traditional materials to the art of fly tying.

The teacher in me enjoyed the chance to share whenever the opportunity presented itself. I decided to not let it overwhelm the rest of my life. It expanded my horizons when I had the chance to develop a T-shirt design and even write this book. Thank you for taking this journey with me.

A Son's Tribute

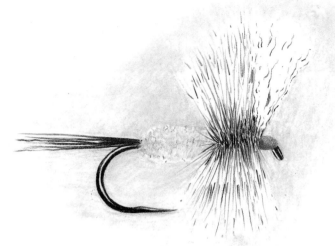

FOR THIS BOOK, MY dad asked me to put on paper some of my thoughts concerning the Clark's Stonefly. I considered the innovative material used for the pattern, the ease of tying the Clark's Stonefly, its versatility and its productivity, but I realized that most of my thoughts regarding this fly revolved around irreplaceable memories of my dad and me together, sharing our love for fly fishing.

My first memory is of the summer when I was ten years old when my dad and I first began hiking on the railroad tracks into the White Horse Rapids area of the Deschutes River. I was equipped with my spinning rod, my dad, his fly rod. For most of the trip, the spinning rod sat propped against a tree unused. I had discovered that my dad's fly rod and fly fishing was more to my taste. After waking from his afternoon naps to find his fly rod missing or his leader stricken with a myriad of wind knots, he was more than willing to purchase my first fly rod. While I didn't understand the basics of fly casting or a drag-free drift, it was clear I had fallen in love with fly fishing. The summer I first developed this passion for fly fishing was also the summer my dad began creating the Clark's Stonefly.

While creation of the Clark's Stonefly began on the Deschutes, it was on the Metolius that my dad perfected the pattern. He would sit in the camper for several hours each day tying stonefly patterns, each one a little different from the last. It was hard for me to understand what he was doing with each variation but I was eager to head off to the river to test each prototype. Come to think of it, I caught fish on every single test pattern! Periodically he would come down to the river, find out how a particular test pattern was working, give me another one to try, and then head back to the camper to create yet another.

The development of the Clark's Stonefly was only the first step in our fly-fishing adventures together. The pattern proved very successful as a salmon and stonefly imitation, but my dad's love of developing new patterns quickly brought about more variations. For example, by varying the color or size of his pattern, it could be transformed into a grasshopper, caddis imitation, or a bass bug. Each variation brought more opportunity to get out on the water and thus more time to spend together. The local bass ponds became a very enjoyable evening outing for us as we tested each new pattern developed.

Fortunately for me, my parents' schedule allowed us to spend most of our summers fishing. Winters were spent as a team; visiting fly shops, tying at sportsman shows, and marketing the Clark's Stonefly. While adult responsibilities and distance have made it difficult to fish together as often as in the past, we still find opportunities to share our love of fly fishing. Whether it's a float down the Deschutes River or a trip to the Northwest Fly Tiers Exposition in Eugene, Oregon, we always manage to find some way to make the fly-fishing connection.

My dad's love of fly tying and fly fishing allowed me to catch more fish in my childhood than most people would catch in a lifetime. For this and the memories of unbelievable nights of fishing on Lost Lake, my first trout on a fly rod, and yearly camping trips on the Metolius and Deschutes rivers, I am forever grateful. But I am most grateful to him for being my dad and for spending time with me. We could have done anything together and I would have been happy. I'm glad it was fly fishing! *—Gerry Clark*

Index

About the Authors

Lee Clark

DON URIE

Over forty years ago, while visiting a grade school class-mate, Lee spotted a beginner's fly-tying kit half hidden on a bedroom shelf. With a whole lot of curiosity, he opened the box and discovered an assortment of bright-colored feathers, hair, and yarn. David, his friend, loaned him the kit for a few days and Lee was hooked. Many hobbies and activities have come and gone but his love of fly tying has continued.

He is a member of the Federation of Fly Fishers, and was chosen the 1989 Fly Tier of the Year by the Oregon Council of the Federation of Fly Fishers. Lee has demonstrated fly tying at many shows over the years, including the International Sportsmen's Exposition in Portland, Oregon and the Northwest Fly Tyers Exposition in Eugene, Oregon.

Lee is also an illustrator, his work has been published in *Flyfishing & Tying Journal* and *Warmwater Flyfishing*. His drawings are also featured in Joe Warren's book, *Tying Glass Bead Flies*.

Lee is a contract fly tier with Umpqua Feather Merchants. He is a retired school teacher and lives in St. Helens, Oregon with his wife, Betty.

Joe Warren

Joe is the author of *Tying Glass Bead Flies* and a freelance writer for fly-fishing and tying magazines. He regularly demonstrates his fly-tying skills at the Northwest Fly Tyers Exposition and the International Sportsmen's Exposition in Oregon. He is currently working on his third book, *Columbia River Flyfishing*.

Joe resides in Carson, Washington with his wife Melissa and daughters, Yoshie, Ashley, and Katy.